Style Your Perfect
WEDDING

Style Your Perfect
WEDDING

Penguin
Random
House

Senior designer Gemma Fletcher

Senior editor Carrie Love

Designers Anne Fisher, Charlotte Johnson,
Lucy Parissi, and Claire Patane

Editors Elinor Greenwood, Jennifer Lane,
Kathryn Meeker, and Laura Palosuo

US editor Margaret Parrish

US senior editor Shannon Beatty

Photographer Charlotte Tolhurst

Stylist Linda Berlin

Production editor Andy Hilliard

Production controller Che Creasey

Senior jacket creative Nicola Powling

US wedding consultant Jody Blomberg

Florists Mark Welford and Stephan Wicks

Managing editor Penny Smith

Managing art editor Marianne Markham

Creative director Jane Bull

Category publisher Mary Ling

First American Edition, 2015

Published in the United States by
DK Publishing
345 Hudson Street
New York, New York 10014

15 16 17 18 19 10 9 8 7 6 5 4 3 2 1
001-256498-Jan/2015

Published in Great Britain by Dorling Kindersley Limited.

A catalog record for this book is available from
the Library of Congress.

ISBN 978-1-4654-2982-7

DK books are available at special discounts when purchased
in bulk for sales promotions, premiums, fund-raising, or
educational use. For details, contact:
DK Publishing Special Markets, 345 Hudson Street,
New York, New York 10014 or SpecialSales@dk.com.

Color reproduction by Alta Image
Printed and bound in Hong Kong by Printing Express Limited

www.dk.com

You are invited to

Style Your Perfect
WEDDING

NAUTICAL

Blush

BOHEMIAN

Garden party

RUSTIC
PAGES 108–133

METROPOLITAN
PAGES 134–153

Vineyard
PAGES 154–175

YOUR WEDDING GUIDE

Introduction

Style Your Perfect Wedding will make the buildup to your wedding as happy and exciting as your relationship. A wedding is a joyful occasion—two people pledging their love and devotion to each other. It is also a stylish one, where the memories you make, and the photos you take, will last you a lifetime together.

Seven wonders

The book is packed full of easy ideas for personal touches and hand-crafted style in seven inspirational themes. Nautical nuptial style is perfect for a coastal celebration. The gorgeous Garden Party is genteel, relaxed, and filled with flowers. Chic, monochrome, Metropolitan style makes an elegant city wedding. Blush is pretty and feminine. The Bohemian theme is artistic, generous, and flooded with color. Rustic is beautiful, natural, and traditional, and Vineyard's lush colors and trailing vines make this an unforgettable wedding theme.

Your reliable assistant

The comprehensive reference section will fill in the blanks in your knowledge. It will help you plan your day to perfection, with time lines for what to do when, as well as ideas and advice on everything—from your invitations to the speeches. With this book on hand, your preparations will go seamlessly, leaving you free to concentrate on the job at hand... getting married to the one you love.

Good luck, all best wishes, and here's to you! Cheers!

NAUTICAL

⚓

BE TRANSPORTED to the seas with this inspired theme. It's all about
dark wood, shiny brass, ship wheels, and blue-and-white stripes.

"*Love* one another but
make not a bond of love:
Let it rather be a
moving sea between
the shores of your souls."
–The Prophet by Khalil Gibran

STYLISH NAUTICAL

CHIC, STYLISH, AND SHIPSHAPE. A nautical wedding is bold and full of wonderful decorations and designs. It's slightly playful, too, with fun options for favors.

COLLECT objects that remind you of the open waters, majestic sailing ships, and sandy shores.

A LIFE BUOY, silky blue ribbon, and striped cloth all steer you strongly in the right direction.

NAVY BLUE, white, teal, red, pale blue, beige, and brown are all ideal colors for this palette.

BRIGHT BLUE flowers express the magnificent beauty of open waters and clear blue skies.

A SHINY wheel key ring, a golden bell, and an antique telescope add depth to this theme.

BILLOWING SAILS on an old book cover convey the buoyant grandeur of a nautical wedding.

The story of
SHIPS
A Ladybird 'achievements' book

NAUTICAL

SHADES OF BLUE AND CREAM create a world of ocean serenity, hinting at bright blue skies, balmy breezes, and calm seas. Clean lines and nautical touches add to the sense of maritime magic.

"My bounty is as *boundless*
as the sea, My *love* as deep;
the more I give to thee, The
more I have, for both are infinite."
~ Romeo and Juliet, 2.2, Shakespeare

PLACE SETTING

CLASSIC SILVERWARE and stylish tableware are ideal for a nautical-themed wedding. Tie napkins in white rope and use a blue-and-white striped tablecloth.

Ambient candles As the sun sets over the sea, candles are a pretty lighting option that will make your venue glow. Coastal wedding parties are often set outside and they catch a welcome cooling sea breeze. These chic takes on the traditional storm lantern are both practical and pretty.

Tasting stars And what better way to toast the sun setting on your wedding day (in fact, to toast *EVERYTHING* on your wedding day) than with champagne? As the Benedictine monk Dom Pierre Perignon said when he invented champagne in the seventeenth century, "Come quickly! I am tasting stars!" Best served chilled.

"The feeling of *friendship* is like that of being comfortably filled with roast beef; *love*, like being enlivened with *champagne*."
–Samuel Johnson

Beautiful blue

Bursting with brightness, blue hydrangeas are bold and beautiful. Fill a variety of vases with varying heights of these striking flowers. Use small bunches of hydrangea as chairbacks at the ceremony and reception. They're also perfect as pew ends.

CHOOSE TWO BLUE
hydrangea heads and tie
them with blue and white
ribbons onto the back of
the chairs for the bride
and groom.

Secrets of the sea

Charming favors Full of seaside appeal, these marine-motif charms make chic coastal wedding favors. Clipped onto key rings, the brass ornaments will be enduring momentos of your nautical nuptials.

Message in a bottle Put messages of love and affection, or favorite quotes from seafaring tales, into mini glass vials. Cork the bottles and add nautical knots to seal in your maritime messages.

Neat and sweet Crisp white boxes tied with striped ribbons and string in shades of indigo are favors with seaside style. Put a sea charm, a special shell, or a chocolate fish inside.

"The voice of the sea speaks to the soul. The touch of the sea is sensuous, enfolding the body in its soft, close embrace."

– Kate Chopin

HELPFUL HINT

When you have tied your bow in the usual way, adjust the length of each loop and trim the ends at an angle for a finished look.

Wheel of good wishes

*HEAD TO COASTAL markets and antique
stores to find authentic items. This
ship's wheel makes a great focal point
and is ideal for displaying guests'
good wishes to the happy couple.*

SCULPT the cork to give it extra texture. A section cut out in the middle looks like a waterway.

Maritime markers

Beautiful boats These boats are simple to make with just a few inexpensive materials. They can be used as seating cards for your wedding guests at the reception tables, or as part of a centerpiece for table numbers. Choose good quality paper or thin card stock.

Cut out a template of your design for a sail, a flag, and a boat. Using a template will keep the display uniform. Cut the pieces out on the fold, then wrap each piece around a toothpick or skewer and glue together. Stick completed boats into loosely knotted light rope or a piece of cork.

NAUTICAL FLOWERS

THIS BOUQUET AND BOUTONNIERE are perfect when you're ready to drop anchor and tie the knot. Ribbons in blue and white stripes are reminiscent of the French Riviera. Blue flowers have an impressive impact when placed next to contrasting bright white flowers. The effect is definitely dramatic.

You will need...

- 5 white roses • 5 cornflowers
- Small bunch of chamomile
- Florist scissors • Florist tape
- String • Blue-and-white striped ribbon

For the bouquet

Step 1 Hold a white rose stem in one hand and add two blue flowers to it. Next, add a few chamomile stems. **Step 2** Continue to fill the bouquet by adding a few flowers at a time. Make sure you distribute the three types of flowers evenly throughout the bouquet. **Step 3** Tie the arrangement at the binding point with string and secure it in a knot. **Step 4** Trim the ends of the stems so they are roughly the same length. **Step 5** Bind the stems together tightly with florist tape. Then cover the florist tape with the blue-and-white striped ribbon from the bottom of the stems to the top. Finish the bouquet with a large, beautifully tied bow.

You will need...

- 1 white rose • 3 rose leaves
- Florist scissors • Florist tape
- Blue-and-white striped ribbon
- White rope

For the boutonniere

Step 1 Cut the rose stem down to about 4in (10cm). Holding the rose leaves around the stem of the rose, wind the florists tape around the stem. This holds the leaves in place. **Step 2** Cover the florist tape in blue-and-white striped ribbon. **Step 3** Tie on a small piece of white rope for an added nautical feel.

HYDRANGEA WREATH

You will need...

Hydrangeas in various shades of blue and cream • Florist scissors • A floral foam ring 10in (25cm) in diameter

How to

Step 1 Immerse the foam ring in water for about three minutes, until no more bubbles rise and the foam is soaked through and feels heavy. Start adding the hydrangeas to the ring. For the inner and outer edges, insert the florets at an upward angle. For the top of the ring, push them in vertically. **Step 2** Build up each section. **Step 3** Fill in any gaps.

THESE BEAUTIFUL
WREATHS make a perfect
surround for a pillar candle
in a glass container. Use
them as centerpieces
for your tables.

STATIONERY

REEL IN YOUR GUESTS with amazing nautical-themed stationery. Your invitation will give them a taste of what's to come, so hook them in with navy blue ribbons and pretty rope trimmings. If you're printing out the text then choose a font reminiscent of an old-fashioned poster advertising the maiden voyage of a cruise liner.

THE APPROACH you use for your invitation is often echoed in the ceremony program, menu cards, seating cards, and thank you cards, so choose a style and font that will work for all of these elements.

Blush

FOR WEDDING STYLE that is pretty, delicate, and feminine, fill your venue with fresh flowers and subtle decorations. The look is perfectly beautiful blush.

"In dreams and in love there are no impossibilities."
- János Arany

Beautiful blush

INSPIRATION FOR THIS THEME comes from tones of pink and peach.
It sets the scene for a beautiful, soft, and natural wedding.

GATHER gorgeous items that inspire the perfect color palette for your wedding.

A VINTAGE perfume spray atomizer adds the lightness of transparent glass to the mix.

CHOOSE objects that are pale pink, peach, pastel green, gold, and cream.

PEACH rose petals offer the element of delicate nature to this theme.

GLIMMERS of gold and soft satin ribbons complement gentle peachy blush.

A TINY work of art—a painting, watercolor, or antique tile—captures the joy of blush.

Blush

SOFT PEACH HUES, TOUCHES OF GOLD, and delicate glassware all work together to create this ethereal and romantic theme. Blush is warm, light, and unashamedly feminine, so opt for sheer fabrics and ribbons, pastel flowers, and soft candlelight.

"But love is blind, and
lovers cannot see
The pretty follies that
themselves commit;
For if they could, Cupid
himself would blush."
–The Merchant of Venice, 2.6

Shakespeare

Place settings

KEEP COLORS SIMPLE,

using shades of light pink and peach.
For understated opulence, choose gold
silverware and gold-rimmed plates.

SELECT TABLEWARE that complements the theme. Bone china plates, delicate wine and water glasses, and a classic glass decanter. They all add to the indulgence of blush.

Floral decorations

GARLANDS OF TANGLED IVY AND ROSES
add to the romance of the wedding and give a secret-
garden feel to the setting. Use these to decorate the
chairs at the head table or at the ceremony.

KEEP ALL OF THE COLORS you use soft. Sticking to a color palette of pink, peach, and cream will ensure that all aspects of the theme link together.

Rose centerpiece

Step 1 Immerse a floral foam block in water for about three minutes, until no more bubbles rise up and the foam is soaked through and feels heavy. Do not oversoak. Trim the corners of the foam with a craft knife, and bind it to a posy vase with floral tape. **Step 2** Lay out flowers and foliage into separate piles of senecio, sedum, pittosporum, roses, aster, and spray roses. Trim the stems of foliage into lengths that will fit into the foam. Insert a stem of senecio into each side of the foam at a downward angle (to hide the base of the posy vase). Add a few stems of senecio in a line across the top of the foam. Insert the stems of sedum to fill the natural spaces in the foam, but leave gaps. **Step 3** Fill in the gaps with the pittosporum, roses, and asters. **Step 4** Insert the spray roses into any extra gaps. **Step 5** Look for obvious spaces in the display and fill them with additional foliage and flowers. Mist the display thoroughly.

Finishing touches

Tables Adorn tables at a blush wedding with delicate lace table runners and soft-pink linen tablecloths. Scatter rose petals over the table, or display the bride's or bridesmaids' bouquets on beautiful pink glass cake stands for an original finishing touch.

Drinks Serve drinks at the reception that echo the theme, adding to the overall atmosphere. Opt for drinks with tones of pink and peach, such as pink champagne, peach cocktails, and rosé wine. Nonalcoholic alternatives are rose petal water and peach cordial.

Glassware Use simple but elegant drinking glasses and glass candleholders to add to the ambience of softness and light. Fill the candlesticks with tall, pale-peach tapers.

"Blushing is the color of virtue."
~Matthew Henry

Fanciful favors

THESE PRETTY FAVOR BOXES are ideal for a blush-themed wedding.
Ask your bridesmaids or family to help you if you're making
lots of favor boxes for a large wedding party.

You will need...

Ready-made favor boxes • Assorted silk ribbons, cut into strips long enough to tie around the boxes
• Small silk flowers on stems • Other embellishments, such as miniature pearls on wire branches
• Tissue paper, cut into squares to fit the size of your favor boxes • Pink and white sugared almonds

How to

Step 1 Lay out all your materials and make sure you have enough of
everything before you begin. **Step 2** Fill a batch of favor boxes with
precut tissue paper. **Step 3** Add enough sugared almonds to fill each box.
Use a mixture of pink and white almonds. **Step 4** Put the lids on the boxes
and tie each one with a bow, mixing and matching the ribbons. Let the ribbon
ends trail, cutting them diagonally to finish. Add flowers to the lids of some
boxes and miniature pearls to others.

Pretty ceilings

TREAT YOUR GUESTS to a vision of grandeur by decorating the ceiling of your wedding

venue with luscious peach, cream, and white paper pom-poms. The pom-poms can

be hung at different heights for variety and interest. In this instance, it's a case of

"more is more." The goal is to fill the whole ceiling of a reception hall

with these incredibly impressive pom-poms.

Packed to the rafters

Paper lanterns An array of Chinese paper lanterns will also create the same effect as pom-poms. Follow the palette from your wedding to choose the correct colors. Pretty pastels or a mixture of light patterns would suit a blush wedding. Be as creative as you want with the amount and the type of decoration. Paper lanterns come in all shapes and sizes, so have fun choosing the right ones for your reception venue.

Floral feature Branch out and try something more natural, such as flower garlands hanging down in plentiful bunches. Twigs and small branches can also be dangled on different lengths of string or ribbon. Create a magical reception room by suspending blossoms for a wedding in the spring or ferns and holly for a winter celebration. For a bit of romance, add some small sprigs of mistletoe to the winter foliage.

Plentiful balloons For fun and impressive decor, use the same principle by suspending multiple balloons from the ceiling. Completely fill the room with balloons in colors to match your blush theme. Mix and match sizes and shapes of balloons. Feel free to intersperse a few subtlely patterned balloons within the single block-colored ones. The overall effect you're aiming for is a visually striking and wonderful display.

Finishing touches

Sparkling space The layout for a blush wedding reception is one of understated beauty. It's refined and regal, while also being artistic and light. A blush room should be composed of romantically themed centerpieces, decor that is deliciously opulent, and amazingly elegant flowers. Everything comes together through softly marrying simple colors and finishes. Gold-rimmed glasses filled with pink champagne sit perfectly on an antique metal serving tray and embody the glamorous sense of blush.

Elegant tables Gold silverware, bone china plates with gold rims, and gold serving pieces all tie together beautifully. Light linen and cloth doilies also enhance the complete feeling of blush. Add a soft, tactile texture to the wedding breakfast table by wrapping gold silverware in peach embroidery thread. The effect is effortlessly glamorous and unique.

Sweet finish Cakes that are perfect for the blush theme include naked cakes, traditional three-tiered frosted cakes, and metallic frosted cakes. For a gold effect, a little sparkle of gold "dust" can be added to a cake by sprinkling fine, edible glitter over the white icing. The glitter adds a decorative sheen to the overall look.

A WEDDING CAKE embossed with a pattern of flowers looks almost too beautiful to eat. This design is particularly perfect for a blush wedding. Another ideal covering is icing that is made to look like lace.

Stationery

LUXURIOUS AND PRETTY, blush is all about being sophisticated, yet subtle. Textured paper, gold and peach thread, and patterned ribbons are all good starting points for your blush wedding stationery. Delicate, blossomlike craft flowers are ideal for attaching to the front of an invitation or menu card. Use a font that looks like the handwriting on an antique love letter. Flowery, flouncy, and formal is the overall feeling you're aiming for.

BOHEMIAN

LOUD, BRIGHT, AND BOLD, an eclectic mix of tableware, patterned fabrics, and trinkets bring this wedding theme to life. Welcome to the world of boho chic.

"Every *heart* sings a *song*, incomplete, until another heart **whispers** back. Those who wish to sing always find a song."
-Plato

BRIGHT BOHEMIAN

A BOHEMIAN WEDDING is bright and bold by design. Make a mood board that creates an air of confidence and coordinates cheerful colors into a perfect mix.

VISIT VINTAGE markets and secondhand stores to pick up treasures for your mood board.

PAINTED TILES, lace-covered embroidery hoops, and an eclectic collection of material all help set the mood.

CHERRY RED, greens, strong purples and pinks, bright yellows, and azure blue all fit the bill.

FLOWERS in vibrant shades fulfill the strong color inspiration for this theme.

A GOLD LUCKY CHARM bracelet echoes the magic of this wedding concept.

A BRIGHTLY PATTERNED tin and a vintage teapot encapsulate the bohemian quirky charm.

BOHEMIAN

SUMPTUOUS, LUXURIOUS, AND BURSTING WITH COLOR, a bohemian wedding provides lasting, vivid memories of a magnificent day. Choose bright objects, strong colors, patterned tableware, and bold decorations.

COLORFUL CONCOCTIONS

A SUMPTUOUS FEAST awaits you
and your guests in a reception room filled
with bright and unusual tableware, all just
right for a bohemian banquet.

A variety of vases

For sumptuous bohemian flower arrangements, use bright pink spray roses and clematis, orange and yellow asclepia, and poppy seed heads. A collection of eclectic vintage tins works well as smaller vases, and each can be used to display a single type of flower.

EMBROIDERY LACE HOOP

You will need...

- Scissors • Wooden embroidery hoops of different sizes • Pieces of lace in a variety of patterns • Brightly colored ribbon (rich purples, fuchsia pink, light pink, gold)
- A selection of bright flowers (sandersonia, pink and orange spray roses, cornflowers)

How to

Step 1 Cut a piece of lace large enough to cover the surface area of the hoop. Unfasten the hoop and lay it out on your work surface. **Step 2** Put the lace over the inner ring and then place the outer ring on top. Adjust the tightness of the ring, pulling the lace until it is taut. Cut off the excess lace. **Step 3** Repeat steps 1 and 2 until you have filled all your embroidery hoops with lace. **Step 4** Tie a long piece of ribbon on to each hoop and suspend each one from the ceiling. Hang the hoops at varying heights. **Step 5** Hang a variety of flowers to accompany the hoops.

Tea for two Brimming with gratitude, a vintage teacup favor looks delightfully boho against a colorful, striped tablecloth. Collect a variety of teacups from vintage stores and antique emporiums. Tied with satin ribbons, they make unique gifts that your guests will enjoy long after the wedding festivities.

Colored candles Bright and beautiful candles will light up your guests' memories of your fantastic party. Choose a color scheme of red, purple, and white to match the rest of the decor, and simply tie and tag with color-coordinating ribbons. Arrange on an etched metal plate for more Moroccan-style boho chic.

COLORFUL GIFT CRACKERS

HAVE FUN experimenting with daring clashes of vivid shades of color to make these packaged gifts for your guests.

How to

Step 1 Lay out a piece of rectangular paper, pattern-side down, and place a narrower piece of white card stock on top. The card stock will create a solid cracker shape. **Step 2** Place your chosen items in the center along the top edge of the card stock. Use candies, marshmallows, or even seed packets. **Step 3** Roll from the top down to the bottom of the rectangle and twist at each end. Tie a piece of string around each end to secure the cracker and finish with a neat bow.

You will need...

Patterned paper
• Card stock
• Your choice of gift
• Scissors • String

TRY LAYERING a mix of light
and sheer textures of paper
to create flowerlike ends.

Out of the ordinary

Spice it up The hot spicy shades of the souk are at the heart of a bohemian theme. Bright hues of pink, purple, and orange, combined with Moroccan-style metal lanterns, will provide a soft glow and an intimate atmosphere. It will put all your guests, and you, in the mood for celebrating love.

Sumptuous relaxing Big floor cushions in hot summer colors with beautiful ethnic fabrics make a boho-chic chill-out zone for guests to enjoy as the evening progresses. For a luxurious touch, treat guests to mint tea as they lounge. Add a few gypsy-style garlands and pretty paper decorations.

"Being deeply loved by someone gives you strength, while loving someone deeply gives you courage."
-Lao Tzu

CHOOSE LANTERNS that are different shapes and sizes. In keeping with the boho theme, everything needs to look mismatched, but at the same time work together.

Freedom of expression

Going boho A bohemian style is an illustration of your perspective on the world. Choosing this theme gives you absolute choice, and an opportunity to display your eclectic mix of style. Be courageous and bold in your decisions on color, pattern, and materials. Confidence is key as you piece together opulent, rich, and unusual items.

Trinket-type tableware Bold vivid colors stand out in this style. Visualize your idyll, perhaps a bustling Moroccan market with polyrhythmic music and aromatic scents. There's no focus on perfection, neat lines, or even softness and subtlety. This is an exploration of draping and layering decorative fabrics, ornate glassware and mismatched eye-catching tableware. Clashing is part of the art.

Eccentricity Let hedonism be your guide. Scatter rose petals of the most vibrant hue across place settings that are busy with candles, colored glass, and metalware. Use brodea, dianthus, and spray roses for a stunning bouquet. Be playful, relaxed, and even a little daring.

"The minute I heard my first love story, I started looking for you. Lovers don't finally meet somewhere. They're in each other all along."
- Rumi

PAPER FAN GARLANDS

THESE PRETTY paper fans create beautiful garlands that are perfect for decorating your venue.

You will need...

An assortment of colorful, patterned paper
• Scissors • Glue stick • White posterboard
• Colorful string

How to

Step 1 Cut your paper into thin strips about 20in (50cm) long. The height can vary, depending on the size fan you want to make. **Step 2** Fold the paper accordion-style until you reach the end. Open out the folded stack to see the fan effect. **Step 3** Hold the ends of the folded paper strip and bring them together to make a circle shape. Glue the edges of the two ends together. For extra strength, stick a circular disk of posterboard on the back of the fan in the middle. **Step 4** Repeat steps 1–3 to make as many fans as you need. Use colorful string to hang all the paper fans against a wall or door. Tape the string to the backs of the fans.

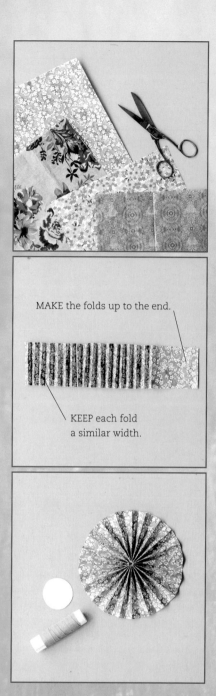

MAKE the folds up to the end.

KEEP each fold a similar width.

STATIONERY

GO BOHO AND LOUD with stationery that proudly shouts color, patterns, and brightness—your guests will be wondering what will await them at the main event. Select individual designs for the invitations and use dark ink to inscribe the information on the inside. Choose brightly colored ribbons to tie ceremony programs into scrolls.

Garden party

ADORN YOUR GARDEN location with hanging flowers and birdcages.
Lawn chairs, green glass, and white linen tablecloths perfect the look.

"*Love* is a canvas
furnished by Nature
and embroidered
by *imagination*."
-Voltaire

Fresh simplicity

GET IN THE MOOD for a garden party wedding. Pick out your favorite floral motifs and vintage garden accessories to capture your distinctive style.

PICK FAVORITE flowers and floral patterns, natural textures, and textiles.

VINTAGE botanical paintings and old floral stamps add an artistic note to the pastoral theme.

TURQUOISE, pink, and yellow with zesty apple green form the ideal color scheme.

OLD-FASHIONED wooden clothes pins and colorful thread have a multitude of wedding uses.

WEATHER-WORN terra-cotta pots pull the look together and lend charm and character.

PAINTED TRAYS offer a vintage vibe that characterizes the pure pleasure of a garden wedding.

Garden party

LOVE IN THE AFTERNOON at a laid-back garden-party wedding is hard to beat.

Lush greenery, soft colors, and vibrant flowers galore are like a breath of fresh air.

Dig in

Capture the essence of summer skies and gardens in bloom with a variety of turquoise and green tableware. Tuck a packet of seeds in with the napkin for place settings with an authentic touch.

SEEDS

Garden of love

Tree decorations Glass jars hung from tree branches with colorful ribbons make delightful handmade details. Use them as containers for tea lights and the day will turn into an enchanted evening. You can also use them as hanging vases to add daytime interest. Match the flowers with your table decorations in striking shades of pink and yellow.

Bright flowers Choose beautiful informal flowers like spray roses, asclepia, and cosmos for your tabletop vases. You can use a variety of pretty glasses to display them. A large birdcage makes a stunning centerpiece. The different styles of container add to the relaxed atmosphere of a garden wedding.

A miniature rose bouquet Strip the thorns from their stems and tie them together with a yellow ribbon for a small decoration with big impact.

"The rose looks fair, but fairer we it deem For that sweet odour which doth in it live."

–Sonnet 54, Shakespeare

MINI BOUQUETS are an extra flower detail perfect for decorating your tables. Alternatively, place the bouquets on the plates of the bridal party.

SCENTED GERANIUM foliage
adds a lovely aromatic touch
to a garden party wedding.

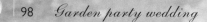

*"The earth laughs
in flowers."*

-Ralph Waldo Emerson

All in the mix

Charming containers Choose old and weather-worn garden accessories and look in secondhand stores for other antique floral touches. An aluminum gardening basket for collecting cut flowers makes a charming container for flower arrangements, and pretty books with floral dust jackets look lovely piled high. Place these in the shade on weathered old chairs for guests to browse. Apple-green linens and rustic, brown-paper seed packets add to the vintage country-garden atmosphere.

Bridal bouquet Choose a mixed variety of spray roses and yellow freesia framed with scented geranium leaves. A garden party will reward you with glowing colors, fragrant smells, and wonderful light. The flowers will look bright and beautiful in this setting.

Chairs and tables A weathered look to the garden furniture makes a perfect backdrop for a charming garden-party wedding. Natural wood and aged metal are a shabby chic choice of seating. Nature does a lot of the decorating work for you. All that is needed is your personal touch to create extra charm and character.

Floral birdcage

You will need...

• White metal birdcage • Florist scissors
• A square block of floral foam, trimmed to fit into
the birdcage • Berried ivy • Spray roses in bright pink
and variegated pink • Asclepia • Cosmos

How to

Step 1 Immerse the foam block in water for
about three minutes, until no more bubbles
rise up and the foam is soaked through and
feels heavy. Do not oversoak. Place the foam
in the bottom of the birdcage. Insert the ivy
into the foam, spacing it out evenly. Work
from the bottom to the top and angle the
stems upward. **Step 2** Then add in the
variegated spray roses. **Step 3** Insert the
bright pink spray roses next. **Step 4** Follow
with the asclepia flowers. **Step 5** The
cosmos should be inserted into the display
last, since it's really delicate. Look for any
obvious gaps in the display
and fill them in.

Wishing tree

A BRANCH FROM A BUDDING APPLE or cherry tree makes a perfect place for guests to hang their best wishes. Buy tags in your color scheme at a stationery store, and provide guests with pencils and pens. Keep the notes (frame them if you like) as wonderful reminders of everyone's warm wishes for you both on your wedding day.

Nature's bounty

Berry bonanza Lush summer berries make popular nibbles, and they look beautiful, too. Arrange them in fruit pallets fresh from the farm and line the pallets with pretty paper napkins.

Straws galore An array of vintage milk bottles filled with different-colored fruit juices will be a magnet for thirsty guests, and they will be greeted with shrieks of delight by children. Colorful, old-fashioned paper straws are a must.

Birdcage table plan Continue the theme by writing guests' names on tags along with their table numbers. Alternatively, use a wire-frame birdcage as a way to collect your guests' comments and best wishes. It will be a "tweet" to read later!

Favorite favors

Cages of color Mini birdcages make intriguing wedding favors, perfect for a garden party. The jewel colors of the tissue wrapping gleam behind ivory bars, and the contrasting-colored satin ribbons tie the gift together nicely. Any lucky bridesmaid or flower girl receiving one of these will be itching to know what's inside. Finish each one with a pretty floral gift tag and message.

Lacy boxes Simple cream boxes are given a pretty lacy look with the clever use of pastel doilies and a piece of blue or pink satin ribbon. Place seed packets inside so memories of the day spring to life later on. Alternatively, you can add chocolates for a sweet treat.

Watch love grow Give your guests packets of seeds of your and the groom's favorite flowers. Whether it's forget-me-nots or sweet peas, guests will enjoy these cheery, charming packets and the dainty blossoms they produce.

Helpful hint

ASK A FLOWER GIRL to hand
out the seed packet favors to
your guests. A woven basket is
the ideal garden-type container
for the job.

Stationery

FLORA AND FAUNA are rich influences for inspiration and feature as decoration on everything from notepads to gift wrap, and wallpaper to greeting cards. This natural selection is a great source of material for your wedding stationery, including invitations, seating cards, and thank-you letters.

RUSTIC

THIS THEME IS INFORMAL and relaxed. Think of a romantic old barn with rustic

wood paneling, white linen with lace edging, and big hay bales for seating.

"*I love* you, not only for *what you are,* but for what I am when I am with you."
- Elizabeth Barrett Browning

ROMANTIC RUSTIC

AN OLD ROMANTIC and rustic barn sets the scene and mood for this theme. Imagine a relaxed party with wooden tables laid out with white linen and beautiful wildflowers.

❋ TAKE A WALK in the countryside to gain inspiration for your rustic-wedding mood board.

❋ SMALL SPRIGS of fresh rosemary tied in a bouquet with brown string add texture and scent.

❋ BUNCHES of wildflowers and fresh herbs help capture the beauty of nature.

❋ CRISP WHITE tablecloths, linen napkins, and lace ribbon all create the desired effect.

❋ CREAMS, whites, browns, and bright green fit the color palette for this theme.

❋ Traditional stationery with watercolor pictures of flowers expresses the delight of rustic.

COUNTRY RUSTIC

SET THE SCENE for a romantic, rustic wedding by keeping everything simple, fresh, and full of character. Favorite antique pieces give a sense of history, while fragrant herbs and wildflowers add the flavor of the countryside.

DELIGHTFUL DINING

SET THE SCENE for a rustic sit-down meal. Make
it a plentiful occasion by using lots of fresh ingredients
and local produce in the dishes you serve.

Decor

Rustic touches Turn back the clock to a simpler time by decorating the venue with a few carefully chosen antiques. Find pieces of country furniture made beautiful by the patina of age. Then arrange them as focal points or display spaces for tin-cup containers of herbs

and flowers, such as cow parsley, mint, alchemilla, marjoram, and chamomile.

Set the scene Bales of hay provide extra seating and evoke the atmosphere of country barn weddings of years gone by. Atmospheric lighting, natural wood, and sheer drapes add depth and texture to

create a wildly romantic rural setting.

Country garland A chamomile garland is made by tying small bunches of the flowers together with string to form a long, draping arrangement. The garland adds to the overall feel of a rustic wedding set in a barn.

Finishing touches

Chair decorations Wildflowers make simple, natural decorations. Choose blooms in colors that blend together. Collect your flowers the day before and keep them in water until the last moment to maintain freshness. String together small bunches of your chosen flowers to create a garland. For the bridal party, make larger bouquets and tie them with natural string or raffia to create decorations for chairbacks.

Additional details Disks of dried tree trunks, pretty jam jars with tea lights, slate, chalk, and as many natural materials as you can use will all add to the countryside feel. Mix textures and materials to add depth to the setting and to create a layered, luxurious feel.

"A flower cannot blossom without sunshine, and a man cannot live without love."
~Max Müller

WILDFLOWER WREATH

DECORATE YOUR VENUE with an inviting wreath. You can make the wreath base ahead of time, but add fresh flowers as close to the event as possible.

You will need...

• Birch twigs • Wire • Chamomile • Mint • Marjoram
• Cow parsley • Florist scissors • String

How to

Step 1 Gather or buy an assortment of flexible branches, such as birch twigs. Weave the branches into a circle using matching wire to hold them at key points.
Step 2 Continue adding branches until you are happy with the overall shape. Work in any loose ends and make sure the wreath is strong and secure.
Step 3 Make small bunches of flowers and tie them together with a piece of string. Make as many bunches as you need to fit around the wreath. **Step 4** Work the bunches of wildflowers in between the branches and secure them in place with the wire or string, if needed.

Pastoral touches

Bring the outdoors in You're likely to choose this charm-filled theme if you are a lover of the great outdoors, comfortable in all things rural, and drawn to the lush, modest beauty of the natural landscape. Think of ways to add natural touches, such as these simple and distinctive burlap silverware pouches. Using a pocket for simple silverware adds shape to your place setting, while providing an opportunity to add natural textures and warmth to your decor. Humble textiles and simple white tableware on raw wood are signature pieces for understated rustic chic.

Lovely lace Add more texture still with delicately embroidered handkerchiefs, folded to create a pocket for wedding favors. Their shape makes them ideal for use as personalized coasters, or as little seed packets of lavender or sweet pea. Find the most elegant lace for tablecloths or table runners. Bare, richly colored wood is visible beneath to add color and character to the reception tables.

Helpful hint

Print a recipe label for the back of the jar or simply list the date and location of your wedding.

Sugar and spice

Fruity favors Homemade preserves made from handpicked fruit from a farm are ideal favors for a homespun wedding. Present them with brown-paper packaging lids and tie them with striped string. Stack the jam jars in a pile on a sweet paper doily that can double as an extra decoration for the venue.

Rustic cake The atmosphere at a rustic country wedding is created by soft lighting, a wooden interior, lace drapes, and pretty table linens. Enhance this natural look with a rustic cake. Place it on a tree-trunk base. Icing made to look like lace—with beads and scattered flowers—perfects the look and feel of the day.

CONFETTI CONES

DISPLAY THESE DAINTY doily cones in a wicker basket or rustic wooden box. Cutout paper shapes work perfectly as confetti.

You will need...

Small paper doilies • Glue stick • Butterfly or heart hole punch
• Old sheet music or newspaper • Sheets of lilac-colored paper • Wicker basket

How to

Step 1 Fold the bottom edge of a paper doily inward to the width of the pattern edging. **Step 2** Make a fold from the top left inward (see below). **Step 3** Next, curl the doily around until it has nearly formed a cone shape. **Step 4** Spread glue on the edge that hasn't been curled in yet. Glue the edge down to form the complete cone shape. **Step 5** Repeat steps 1–4 for as many confetti cones as needed. **Step 6** Punch hundreds of heart or butterfly shapes out of sheet music or newspaper. Fill the confetti cones with the paper hearts or butterflies.

"A *happy* marriage is a
long **conversation** which
always seems too short."
-André Maurois

RUSTIC LADDER

You will need...

Brown card-stock gift tags • Heart-shaped stamp

Black ink stamp pad • Wooden ladder • Small wooden clothespins

Brown string • Vintage pitcher • Vintage tin cup • Small glass cup or vase

• Nigella • Chamomile • Scabious • Astrantia

How to

Step 1 (before your wedding) Lay out a batch of luggage tags and stamp a heart shape onto one side of each. Set aside to dry. **Step 2 (on your wedding day)** If you're using the ladder as a place for guests to leave messages, set it up in a corner where there is room for people to stand nearby and write their notes. Add a sign to make it clear why the ladder is there. Alternatively, place the ladder at the front of the reception room as the place where guest can find their table number. **Step 3** Hang lines of string across the ladder. Attach the gift tags to the string using wooden clothespins. **Step 4** Add the finishing touches... a bunch of chamomile, a vintage pitcher, and a tin filled with lovely wildflowers.

Helpful hint

This beautiful rustic ladder is a wonderful decorative piece for your wedding venue. It can be used as a seating plan guide or as a place for guests to leave messages for the couple. Decorate it with nigella, "love in the mist," a particularly lovely flower for a wedding.

STATIONERY

PRETTY PAPER DOILIES and dainty ribbon form perfect decorations for rustic wedding invitations and RSVP cards. Luggage tags, brown paper, and card stock are all ideal and help create the look of an old-fashioned package. Stamp hearts on to your save-the-date cards to lift your stationery above everyday mail and use lace edging around your menu cards or ceremony programs.

"We are all born for love. It is the principle of existence, and its only end."

~ Benjamin Disraeli

SOPHISTICATED METROPOLITAN

PICTURE AN ELEGANT 1920s-inspired wedding set in a modern city to help create your vision. A metropolitan wedding is chic and sophisticated.

- DINE or have drinks in a top-notch city restaurant. Take in the decor and study the menu.

- BLACK, white, bright pink, and shades of cream are all fitting for a Metropolitan palette.

- SPARKLY JEWELRY provides a touch of elegance that's utterly necessary for this theme.

- A BLACK-AND-WHITE striped table runner is an ideal backdrop for your mood board.

- BRIGHT PINK classic roses bring a burst of energy to a monochrome color scheme.

- A COCKTAIL GLASS with a metallic finish reflects the grand occasion of Metropolitan.

METROPOLITAN

THIS DRAMATIC COLOR SCHEME has a touch of twenties glamour. Single-color roses bring an explosion of shocking pink to contrast elegantly with black-and-white linen.

THE TOAST
OF THE TOWN

SLEEK AND STYLISH, a monochrome palette
is perfect for an elegant city wedding. Cut glass
adds to the sense of occasion.

Finishing touches

STARK WHITE PLATES with
black rims make stylish
frames around each course.

"Love does not consist of gazing at each other, but in looking outward together in the same direction."
—Antoine de Saint-Exupéry

City sleek

Fans metro style Simply fold some pretty papers in black-and-white accordion style. Make a hole and thread a ribbon through it to make these fashionable fans, which will keep your guests cool on hot city nights.

Table planning Sleek and sharp is key to metropolitan style. This geometric and monochrome table plan with headings that are pink roses is structural and textured. Make it by cutting out the white cards and gluing them onto a black-and-white striped background. Poke the roses through and attach on the back.

TABLE PLAN

Justin Scott
Sylvia Ward
Brandon Flores
Clarissa Jones
Michael Jones
Anna Jones

Douglas Cook
Justin Peterson
Miriam Delaney
James Love
Patricia Love
Sally Cohen

Christina Brown
Martha Rogers
Ruby Miller
Peter Morales
Elizabeth Bailey
Sam Bailey

Pete Ward
Henny Smith
Gemma Fera
Bledi Fera
Tim Carey
Michelle Carey

Ethan Hughes
Lydia Chen
Maria Martinez
Sandy Mitchell
John Mitchell
Derek Washington

Patrick Perry
Emilia Cruz
Thomas Jackson
Mary-Jo Moore
Sara Thomas
Ben Thomas

Allison Levin
Louis Harris
Rose Taylor
Mike Taylor
Denise White
Austin White

Peter Duffy
Christeen Duffy
Jeremy Greenwood
Annabel Greenwood
Amber Walker
Roger Hill

Nelson Gatsby
Bee Robinson
Louis Allen
Sarah Allen
Maxine Hall
Charlie Campbell

METROPOLITAN ROSES

THESE ARRANGEMENTS are perfect for the table centerpieces and can be given to the bridal party as gifts.

You will need...

- Floral foam • Knife
- A sheet of cellophane • Rectangular planter
- Florist scissors • Kitchen scissors
- 8 pink roses

The foam needs to be wet enough to keep the roses hydrated.

How to

Step 1 Immerse the foam in water for about three minutes, until no more bubbles rise up and the foam is soaked through and feels heavy. Don't let it soak longer. Using a knife, carefully cut the foam down to fit the planter. **Step 2** Place the cellophane in the planter, followed by the foam. Trim the cellophane so that it's just below the top of the planter. The cellophane keeps the planter watertight. **Step 3** Use florist scissors to cut the rose stems down to a height that will fit into the depth of the foam in the planter. Insert the roses into the foam block. **Step 4** Place the last few roses into the foam block to complete the rose arrangement.

Other arrangements

TO MAKE THE SUCCULENT *arrangements, place cellophane in a rectangular or cubed planter, then fill it nearly to the rim with multipurpose compost. Make two small holes in the soil. Plant an echeveria succulent in each hole. Make sure the plants are evenly spaced.*

Witty and pretty

Glass candlesticks Witty and fun details bring metropolitan style to life. These up-ended wineglasses, with pink roses peeking out, make quirky candlesticks to go with the theme. Pillar candles in different heights adorned with black ribbon look city-chic and will light up the party with a soft glow.

Showstopper cake A white-iced layer cake looks elegant with sugar flowers with black centers cascading from the top. A pure white rose tied with black-and-white ribbon adds to the sweetly stunning design. The wedding cake is artfully arranged on a boldly-striped tablecloth echoing the monochrome color scheme. Twinkling fairy lights behind make a charming backdrop and will look great in your photos. When you cut into this showstopping beauty you'll feel like the king and queen of New York!

SPLIT YOUR VENUE into different zones, all with a black and white theme and pink highlights. The wedding cake deserves to be styled separately to best frame its beauty.

"*Let me be surrounded by luxury, I can do without the necessities!*"

-Oscar Wilde

PLANT your succulents in glossy black cups, adorned with a bright pink ribbon. For an even more personal gift, propagate your own plants and care for them until the big day.

Fun favors

Sip and savor Chic little bottles of sparkling wine served with stylish monochrome straws will go down well with your guests. They make fun favors that are full of wit and charm. Add a message to the label, such as the date and location of your wedding. Simply tie with string... and cheers! Here's to you!

Pots of style Cup-sized succulents are always in style and make sweet favors. There are over 100 different types and they look stunning arranged together. They are the perfect plant—exotic, easy to care for, and super stylish. Your guests will treasure theirs, along with the memories of your happy day.

STATIONERY

THE IDEAL STATIONERY for a metropolitan wedding echoes that of a premier city hotel or restaurant. Place your stylish, classic invitations in sleek black envelopes and secure them with silver wax seals.

Sealed with a wax flower

WAX STICKS and stamps are easy to use and make a big impact. They can feature as the header for a menu card or as a seal on an envelope. Choose a stamp design that works for the theme, such as a classic rose. Have a trial run using the stamp on a piece of blank paper to make sure you've got the hang of it.

Helpful hint

A BLACK-AND-WHITE color scheme works for invitations, ceremony programs, seating cards, and menus. Use a silver-patterned ribbon for decoration or to tie ceremony programs into scrolls.

Vineyard

PLAN A PARTY TO REMEMBER. Create vineyard luxury with centerpieces of grapes and vine leaves. Delicious olives, fresh figs, and luscious wine add to the mood of indulgence.

"The madness of love is the greatest of heaven's blessings."
—Plato

Luscious vineyard

A VINEYARD WEDDING is rich, opulent, and luscious. Make a mood board that sets the scene for a sophisticated and beautiful wedding.

❀ VISIT A VINEYARD to help fill your mood board with authentic items and ideas.

❀ WOODEN cheese boards and an antique cheese knife assist you with setting the right tone.

❀ DEEP PURPLES, olive greens, teal, and violet are all ideal colors for a vineyard wedding.

❀ BURGUNDY and purple wildflowers enliven and enrich the scope of the mood board.

❀ AN OLD CORKSCREW and wine corks bring in the elements of a real vineyard.

❀ A GLASS BOTTLE and a classic wine glass capture the pure enchantment of a vineyard.

Vineyard

DEEP, LUSH, EARTHY TONES are the
defining characteristic of a vineyard
theme. Use wine as your guide;
burgundies mixed with
rich foliage and
perfectly ripe fruits
set the scene.

Place settings

PLAN YOUR PLACE
SETTINGS to evoke the image
of fall in a French farmhouse.
Use rustic touches, simple but
beautiful glassware, and flora
from the natural landscape.

Finishing touches

PLUMP, RIPE FRUIT and seasonal flowers
echo the wine-rich colors of your theme.

Bridal bouquet

You will need...

Astrantia • Clematis • Lilac rose • Corylus • Florist scissors
• String • Ribbon • Decorative pins

How to

Step 1 Strip any excess leaves from the bottoms of the stems and trim them to the same length. Arrange the flowers into piles by type. Choose a focal flower for the center of the bouquet. Hold the flowers at the binding point, as shown in the image.

Step 2 Keeping the bouquet upright, continue adding flowers and pieces of greenery around the central flowers.

Step 3 Once you are happy with the bouquet, add pieces of greenery around the flowers to frame it. Securely tie the stems together with string. **Step 4** Wrap the ribbon around the string. Gently place the bouquet down on your worktop. Use a pin to secure the end of the ribbon in place.

Helpful hint

As an added piece of decoration, push pins at an upward angle into the ribbon and stems to form a bunch of grapes.

Boutonnieres

You will need...

- Assorted flowers and greenery • Florist scissors
- String • Raffia or ribbon

How to

Step 1 Arrange a small assortment of flowers and greenery into a miniature bouquet, adjusting it until you are happy with the look. Use flowers and greenery in a variety of heights, placing taller pieces at the back. **Step 2** Carefully tie string around the stems to hold them in place. **Step 3** Check that you are happy with how the boutonniere will look by holding it up to a jacket. If you're not happy, take it apart and try again. **Step 4** Tie the boutonniere securely with a neat knot or bow using the string or raffia. Cover the string or raffia with ribbon if you like. Trim the ends of the string, raffia, or ribbon. **Step 5** Trim the stems of the flowers and greenery. To keep them hydrated, place them in a teacup with a small amount of water. Don't allow the string, raffia, or ribbon to get wet.

Flowers and more

Floral arrangements Use rustic and robust garden urns as vessels for your flowers. Using classic garden pieces helps maintain the theme so you and your guests feel as though you're wandering through a vineyard, even inside the venue.

Candles For an elegant addition to the tables, wrap freshly picked leaves around simple white candles and secure with natural twine. Use pillar candles that burn slowly and try a variety of sizes for a relaxed, natural-looking glow.

"Wine enters through the mouth, Love, the eyes. I raise the glass to my mouth, I look at you, I sigh."
- W. B. Yeats

Table decor

Centerpieces and seating cards are key features and perfect tools for displaying this theme's opulent, luxurious feel. And since they have a practical purpose, you can be sure your guests will notice them. To make the wine cork seating cards, simply begin collecting corks, or get in touch with a local restaurant or bar and ask them to save some for you. Score a line in the top and slot in your card. The card can be simple, as it is above, or with more color and decoration—as you wish. A small dot of reusable adhesive on the bottom will keep the seating cards from falling out.

A bold, towering centerpiece of wine bottles, flowers, and fruit encapsulates the lavish style required, and it can be gradually and indulgently consumed by guests throughout the meal.

Table 8

Rosemary gifts

ROSEMARY is the perfect present to give as a favor at a vineyard wedding. It's aromatic and long-lasting and your guests will remember the occasion every time they use the herb in their cooking.

Olive oil favors

Step 1 Fill miniature swing-top glass bottles with olive oil. **Step 2** Glue a burgundy silk ribbon onto each bottle. **Step 3** Make a personalized red seal for each bottle by melting sealing wax and imprinting it with a design. **Step 4** Glue a wax seal on top of the ribbon on each bottle.

Stationery

DECORATE YOUR STATIONERY to make it look like it's from a vineyard. Use fonts and calligraphy that you would find on wine bottle labels. Artificial leaves and flowers make beautiful embellishments for invitations, menu cards, and seating cards. Add deep purple ribbon, rippled or rolled, to create a sense of richness and ripeness on your stationery.

YOUR WEDDING GUIDE

AN ELEGANT EXPERT guide to planning and styling your perfect wedding,
with information and advice on everything you need to know.

18-MONTH TIME LINE

THE AVERAGE ENGAGEMENT lasts around 18 months. If you're planning your wedding in this time frame, follow the time line below to find out what lies ahead. Create an online calendar and fill it with reminders and alerts for when to complete certain tasks.

12–18 months before
• Choose a wedding date. The earlier, the better!
• Decide on your budget.
• Start a wedding file and an online mood board.
• Agree on what kind of wedding you want (Formal or informal, big or intimate, church or town hall?).
• Select venues for both the ceremony and reception, or book a tent.

8–12 months before
• Start shopping for your dress.
• Decide on a theme or style you like.
• If you're having a destination wedding, send out your save the date one year in advance.
• Book with the wedding official/registrar.
• Choose your best man, maid of honor, bridesmaids, ring bearer, flower girl, and ushers.
• Hire a caterer.
• Choose your wedding cake.
• Contract the photographer.
• Book the band or DJ (or both!).
• Decide on bridesmaid dresses.
• Choose what the men will wear.
• Book a florist.
• Hold an engagement party.

5–7 months before
• Finalize the guest list.
• Order your wedding stationery (or start making your own).
• Book a place to stay for your first night as Mr. and Mrs.
• Book your honeymoon.
• Sign up for a wedding gift registry.
• For non-destination weddings, send out save the dates six months in advance.
• Book hairdresser and makeup artist, if required.

4 months before
• Shop for wedding rings.
• Choose the bride's wedding shoes and accessories.
• Get any vaccinations you might need for an exotic honeymoon.

3 months before
- Send out your invitations.
- Book your transportation to and from the ceremony.
- Discuss final menu, drink options, and costs with caterer.
- Order, or begin making, your wedding favors.
- Shop for bridal party gifts.
- Begin any necessary sessions with wedding officials.
- Finalize venue details—table decorations, timings, etc.

2 months before
- Book a venue for the rehearsal dinner.
- Choose music, readings, and vows for the ceremony.
- Schedule alterations and fittings for the bridal party.
- Confirm your order with the florist or order the flowers if making the bouquets yourself.

1 month before
- Apply for your marriage license.
- Have a final dress fitting.
- Try out your hair and makeup.
- Contact any guests who haven't replied.
- Give the caterers the final head count.

2 weeks before
- Pick up your marriage license and obtain any legal information.
- Give the DJ or band a list of favorite songs, as well as a list of any songs you do not want played.
- Confirm the rehearsal plans.
- Complete the seating plans.
- Confirm all rental and floral delivery dates and times.
- Confirm arrival time for all attendees.
- Break in your wedding shoes (indoors) so you can enjoy the day pain-free.

1 week before
- Make any last-minute seating adjustments.
- Make and print your wedding day programs.
- Give the best man and maid of honor lists of everything they need to do on the day.
- Confirm honeymoon reservations.
- Confirm hotel reservations for guests.
- Pack for your honeymoon.
- Prepare passports and other travel documents.
- Confirm head count and reservation for rehearsal dinner.
- Pick up all rented formalwear.

The day before
- Go through the plans and make sure everyone knows what they are doing, and when.
- Make a wedding day emergency kit (makeup, tissues, eye drops...).
- Put together your bouquet if making it yourself.
- Get all the wedding clothes ready.
- Give the rings to the best man.
- Have a manicure and pedicure and relax!
- Hold the rehearsal dinner.
- Sleep well!

Wedding day
- Eat a decent breakfast.
- Have your hair and makeup done.
- Ask someone to check the reception venue.
- Get dressed for the big occasion.
- Remember your bouquet.

6-MONTH TIME LINE

A SHORT ENGAGEMENT doesn't mean you can't have the wedding you've always dreamed of. Follow the time line below to help your planning run smoothly. There's a lot to do even for the simplest weddings, so being organized is key. Remember, your friends and family will be only too glad to help and give advice.

As soon as possible
- Agree on a budget.
- Decide on the number of guests and make a list.
- Pick your date. You might need to be flexible, depending on venue and supplier availability. Consider a nontraditional day, such as a Friday.
- Choose a theme and a color scheme.
- View and book a venue, or a tent.
- Book the church/ceremony.
- Book with the town hall.
- Send out save the dates as soon as your date and venue are confirmed. Consider paperless options.

- Buy your dress. You may need to pay extra for a rush order from a traditional bridal shop. Consider off-the-rack options or find sample sales. There are many websites where you can buy designer wedding dresses secondhand too.
- Book your photographer, caterer, band/DJ, and florist.
- Choose the best man, maid of honor, ushers, bridesmaids, and ring bearers.
- Choose and order bridesmaids' dresses and pick out what the men will wear. If you're very short on time, consider giving the bridesmaids a specific, easy-to-find color, such as navy, and asking them to buy a dress of their choice. You can then buy them matching accessories.
- Order your wedding invitations and other stationery (or start making your own).
- Order the cake.

5 months before
- Sign up for a wedding gift registry.
- Hold an engagement party or dinner.
- Book a hairdresser and makeup artist, if required.
- Book your honeymoon.
- Book a place to stay for your first night as Mr. and Mrs.

4 months before
- Shop for wedding rings.
- Choose the bride's wedding shoes and accessories.
- Get any vaccinations you might need for an exotic honeymoon.

The last 3 months
Follow the time line on page 179.

Beauty timeline

MAKE SURE YOU'RE FEELING your best on the day of your wedding. Avoid any potential mishaps by trying out products and your hair and makeup well in advance.

Beauty bag essentials

- Sunscreen
- Mints
- Toothpaste and toothbrush
- Dental floss

- Lipstick and lip balm
- Hairbrush and comb
- Powder
- Foundation
- Cotton swabs
- Tissues
- Adhesive bandages and gel heel cushions
- Medicine (paracetemol, indigestion tablets, aspirin)
- Deodorant

- Sanitary items
- Hairspray
- Bobby pins and hair ties
- Hand sanitizer
- Nail polish
- Nail file

ONE YEAR BEFORE

• Consult a dermatologist if you have any issues that you want to remedy.
• Decide if you're going to do your own hair and makeup, or if you're going to ask a professional to do it.

EIGHT MONTHS BEFORE

• Start your exercise plan.
• Begin taking daily multivitamins.
• Start drinking lots of water every day. Being hydrated does wonders for your skin.
• Begin trying different hair and makeup styles. Play around with different colors and brands if you're going to do your own makeup.
• Begin mastering your skin-care routine. Whatever your skin-care routine is on the day of your makeup tryout, the same should be followed for your wedding day so that they match.

FIVE MONTHS BEFORE

• Look at bridal magazines for inspiration.
• Watch online tutorials if doing your own makeup.

FOUR MONTHS BEFORE

• Experiment with self-tanning products to find the right one.
• Decide on your hair and makeup and get everything booked, especially if you have a particular stylist you want to use.

THREE MONTHS BEFORE

• Consider having a facial. You should be making sure your skin is looking and feeling good.

ONE MONTH BEFORE

• Try using a teeth whitening gel. It gives you a shiny smile and takes years off your face. Or you can get your teeth professionally whitened, if necessary.
• Shop for beauty items and order any that aren't available in stores.
• Attend your final makeup and hair trials.

TWO WEEKS BEFORE

• Get your hair trimmed and your roots colored, if needed.
• Confirm that all your bookings are still in place.
• DO NOT experiment with any new products after this date.

ONE WEEK BEFORE

• Sort out all your waxing needs.
• Avoid carbonated drinks, salty foods, or anything that you know makes you bloated.
• Get a gentle facial. Don't have any more facials after this day.
• Avoid excessive sunshine. You don't want a sunburn or tan lines.
• Put together a beauty bag of essentials. See the list, left.

THREE DAYS BEFORE

• Deep condition your hair and have a massage.
• Give yourself a healthy glow by getting a fake tan.

ONE DAY BEFORE

• Have a manicure and pedicure.
• Wash your hair. Hair that is one day dirty will take to a hairstyle better than hair that's just been washed.

THE NIGHT BEFORE

• Make sure you get 8–10 hours of beauty rest and keep yourself hydrated. Take a bath and relax.

THE WEDDING DAY

• Have a shower about 4–5 hours before you get into your wedding dress.
• Have your hair and makeup done.
• Double-check your manicure and moisturize your hands.
• Spritz perfume on yourself just before you leave.

BUDGETING

FIRST THING'S FIRST, decide together on your total budget... and decide to stick to it! These pages show you what you need to budget for when you're planning and paying for your wedding.

WEDDING DAY BUDGET PIE

Whatever your budget, you want to make sure you have one. This wedding pie provides a guide that you can adapt to suit you. Some slices may be bigger or smaller, as long as you keep to the overall cost. This is just a wedding day budget. There are also the bachelor and bachelorette parties, engagement party, engagement ring, rehearsal dinner, first night accommodation, and honeymoon. The average honeymoon is the equivalent to a fifth of what you spend on your wedding day. Of course, it's completely up to you what you save or splash out on! There are spreadsheets you can use and tools you can download to aid you in working out your budget and monitoring your spending. Bear in mind that nonrefundable deposits are often required for the venue, caterer, photographer, florist, and the videographer.

Wedding day budget: suggested percentages

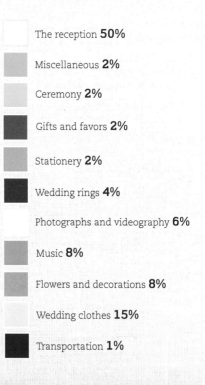

- The reception **50%**
- Miscellaneous **2%**
- Ceremony **2%**
- Gifts and favors **2%**
- Stationery **2%**
- Wedding rings **4%**
- Photographs and videography **6%**
- Music **8%**
- Flowers and decorations **8%**
- Wedding clothes **15%**
- Transportation **1%**

THE WEDDING RECEPTION (50%)

Venue
Rentals
Caterers
Drinks
Wedding cake

WEDDING CLOTHES (15%)

The bride's dress (and alterations)
Groom's outfit
Attendants' outfits
Bride's accessories
Hair and makeup

FLOWERS AND DECORATIONS (8%)

Flowers
Bride's bouquet
Flower girls' and bridesmaids' bouquets
Boutonnieres
Corsages
Reception decorations
Lighting

MUSIC (8%)

Ceremony musicians
Reception music
Band/DJ
Sound system or dance floor rental

PHOTOGRAPHS AND VIDEO (6%)

Photography
Videography

GIFTS AND FAVORS (2%)

Welcome gifts for out-of-town guests
Bridal party gifts
Favors for all the guests

CEREMONY (2%)

Site fee
Wedding official's fee or church donation

STATIONERY (2%)

Save-the-date cards
Invitations and RSVP cards
Wedding day programs
Seating cards
Menu cards
Thank-you notes
Postage

WEDDING RINGS (4%)

Bride's ring
Groom's ring

TRANSPORTATION (1%)

Limo or car rental for bride and groom
Limo or car rental for bridal party
Transportation for guests

MISCELLANEOUS (2%)

For things you didn't budget for (there's always something!)

Tips and ideas for saving money

You can be incredibly creative with your wedding budget and save money in many ways.

Ask for discounts and be willing to negotiate with suppliers on getting extras added in.

Make your own favors and stationery.

Ask relatives and friends to help make things. Perhaps someone handy with a sewing machine can make your dress or you might know someone who can bake and decorate your wedding cake.

Cut out anything from the list that you don't feel is necessary for your wedding. For example, you could do your own playlist for the ceremony and reception music.

Save the date

When it comes to inviting your nearest and dearest to your wedding, there are certain rules you should follow. If you want to make sure people are around for your big day then you need to give them advance notice in the form of a "save the date."

> *"... that sanguine expectation of happiness which is happiness itself."*
>
> ~Jane Austen

You're engaged and you've set a date for your big day. You've booked the venue for your ceremony and reception. You're excited and can't wait—now is the time to tell everyone about it. The best way to do this is through a save-the-date notice.

If your wedding is in the summer or if you're planning a destination wedding then it's worth sending out advance warning a year before, especially if your guests are from out of town. Otherwise, six to eight months should suffice. It all depends on the time you have to plan your wedding. Just don't send notices out too soon or people might lose them.

There are a variety of ways to make your announcement, but before you do so, make sure you've decided exactly who will be invited to your ceremony and/or evening party. Here is a range of ideas that you can use to let your guests know they will be invited to your wedding and therefore need to keep the date free.

PINS

You can buy a make-your-own pin kit to create a pin with your save-the-date information. You can also have these professionally made.

MAGNETS

A classic save-the-date reminder is a magnet that guests can put on their fridges. How you design your magnet is up to you. There are companies that print them relatively cheaply. You can use a photo of you and your groom-to-be on the magnet, along with the date of your wedding.

PHOTOS

Couples often have engagement shots done by a professional photographer. You can have a selection of these images printed on a postcard or on photographic paper. Send them out to everyone in pretty envelopes.

TAGS

Luggage tags make ideal wedding save-the-date items. Handwrite them yourself or get them printed. Choose a plain color for the tag and then add a ribbon or decorative string.

FLOWERS

Decorate your save-the-date cards with delicate dried flowers. Glue a few to the front of each card. Again, this is time-consuming, so probably best for a smaller wedding.

CARDS

Beautiful stationery can be used in many ways to create personalized and pretty save-the-date cards. It's a wonderful way to announce to everyone that you're going to get married on a certain date.

ARTWORK

It's easy to buy miniature canvases on easels in bulk. If you're a budding artist you can paint your save-the-date information onto the canvases. Bear in mind it's a labor of love and incredibly time-consuming. This might work best for a smaller wedding.

COASTERS

It's great if you can make your save-the-date reminder a bit unusual, since it will definitely stick in everyone's minds. Cardboard coasters are a fun way to be different. Choose the image and text you want to use and simply upload them to a site that makes coasters.

INVITATION FOLDS

THERE ARE MANY OPTIONS when it comes to choosing the style of your invitations. You can have a single card with inserts, different folds, or pockets.

RECTANGLE

Classic and popular, a rectangular invitation can be easily embellished or left to stand on its own.

SQUARE

These are incredibly versatile; include a few square cards with various details on each one.

TEA LENGTH

Slim and chic, tea length invitations say modern elegance.

GATE FOLD

Offering lots of space and options, a gate-fold hides the main details, offering an element of surprise.

POCKET FOLD

Practical and a little quirky, pocket-fold invitations keep all the details and any inserts neatly together.

TRI-FOLD

Giving you six sections, front and back, a tri-fold invitation gives you ample space to fit all of the details.

HALF FOLD WITH POCKET

Many folded options are available with a pocket inside to hold extra inserts you might have. This will help guests to keep everything together.

HALF FOLD

Classic half-fold invitations can be very simple, or dressed up, depending on the optional extras and design you choose.

Top tip

Most printers will provide samples of their papers and ink. Once you've narrowed your preferences, order some to check you are happy with the quality and colors before spending money on the real invitations.

EMBELLISHMENTS

IN ADDITION TO THE CARD, your invitations can also be personalized with extra touches, such as ribbons, bands, and seals. These add texture and depth.

CORNER RIBBON
An accent ribbon on opposite corners can add a simple pop of color.

TAG
Set out extra-important information on a tag, or just use a design, your names or initials, or the date.

SEAL
You can add a personal seal to the back of the envelope or around the invitation itself on a belly band.

BELLY BAND
A paper or ribbon band can be put around the invitation. This can be decorative or contain information.

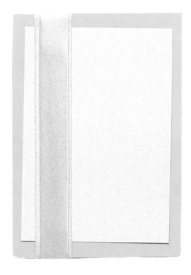

ACCENT RIBBON
A plain invitation can be dressed up with an accent ribbon in your wedding color.

BOW
A simple ribbon tied in a bow through the top can act as a decoration, or can hold layers together.

FORMAL INVITES

WEDDING INVITATIONS ARE OFTEN KEPT AS MEMENTOS by you and by your guests, so you want to make them beautiful and special. They serve a more practical purpose, too, since they contain all the details of your big day.

The hosts

TRADITIONALLY, the parents of the bride are the hosts listed at the top of the invitation. Use the word "honor" if the ceremony is taking place in a house of worship or "pleasure of your company" if the venue is secular. When divorced parents are hosting, list them on separate lines. Do not use "and" to connect their names.

The date and time

IT'S NOT NECESSARY to include the year, but if you decide to, then write it out in full, using an uppercase letter for the first word. Clearly spell out the time the ceremony starts.

Mr. and Mrs. John Davies
request the honor of your presence
at the marriage of their daughter

Katherine
to
Mr. Andrew
William Hunt

Saturday the twenty-third of February
Two thousand and fourteen
at four o'clock in the afternoon

City Church
San Francisco

Reception to follow

The couple

ON A CEREMONY invitation use the connecting word "to" for the couple being wed, unless they are Jewish or Catholic, in which case use the joining word "and."

The location

LIST THE VENUE followed by the location on the next line of text.

Additional advice

1 When the couple is hosting the wedding, use the wording "...invite you to share in their wedding."

2 When both sets of parents are hosting, list the bride's parents first, followed by the groom's.

3 If the couple and both sets of parents are hosting then say "Together with their parents...."

4 For a widow, use "...requests the honor of your presence at the marriage of her daughter."

5 Ask a friend with a good eye for detail to spell-check all the names and wording on the invite.

6 It's important to double- and triple-check all the information is correct before printing your invites.

WHO ARE THE HOSTS?

Traditionally, the hosts listed on the invitation are the bride's parents, since they were the ones who paid for the wedding. Today, many couples pay for their own weddings or receive financial assistance from one or both sets of parents. The invitation needs to reflect this by listing the relevant people as the hosts.

WHEN DO YOU SEND OUT INVITATIONS?

Invitations are generally sent out six to eight weeks before the big day. Get your invitations weighed and make sure you put enough postage on invitations to avoid any delays.

WHO ARE YOU INVITING?

Make it clear who you are inviting to the wedding. If you want a single friend to bring a "plus one" then make it clear. If your friends or family have children and you don't want to invite them, then make this obvious by just listing the names of the parent(s). If someone returns a response card with a child's name on it, too, then call and politely say that children are not invited. This is also something you can put on your wedding website.

HOW TO ADDRESS YOUR GUESTS

• Spell out all the names on the envelope.

• Do not use abbreviations (except for those such as Jr. and Dr.)

• Even when the children are invited, the envelope should only be addressed to the parents. The names of the children should be listed on the invitation itself in age order, with the oldest child's name first.

• If you're inviting a guest with a plus one, try to obtain the contact details for the additional guest and send them an invitation too.

• Include an RSVP card and stamped and addressed return envelope if your budget allows.

WEDDING LISTS

Traditionally, a wedding list was to help a couple get all the items they needed to set up a home together. A lot of couples today ask for money or they have a very specific gift registry at their favorite department store. According to wedding etiquette, this is something best left off the invitations, but can be included on an insert or on your wedding website.

WEDDING WEBSITE

The majority of couples set up a website. This enables you to provide the following information:

• Maps and directions for getting to the wedding and ceremony.

• Gift registry for a particular store.

Couples may ask for any monetary gifts to be donated to a charity or toward paying for the honeymoon.

• Information on how to RSVP.

• Suggestions for accommodation for the night of the wedding (hotels, guest houses, and B&Bs). Couples are sometimes able to negotiate a special deal with a nearby hotel.

CHOOSING YOUR VENUE

CHOOSING THE RIGHT VENUE is not an easy decision because it's such an important part of the day. Take the time to consider all of your options.

REMEMBER YOUR BUDGET

What can you actually afford? Are you willing to go slightly above your budget for a dream location? Keep in mind that certain venues offer cheaper rates for weekdays or unpopular dates, such as Friday the 13th. It's possible to get last-minute deals if venues have cancellations, but this can be a risky approach. Don't be afraid to ask about discounts.

WHEN?

Some venues are booked solid two years in advance. If there's a location you really want for a certain date, then you'll need to think ahead. If you're flexible about dates, then you'll have more options. Consider the time of day you want to get married. Do you want an all-day event, or are you happy just to have an evening event? You'll need to provide drinks and hors d'oeuvres in between different parts of the day, so consider this when budgeting. Also, timing can be key if you're getting married in a place of worship. Are there restrictions on how long you can have the location or are there other events scheduled for the same day?

DESTINATION WEDDINGS

Weddings in far-flung places can sometimes be cheaper than weddings closer to home because you can expect fewer guests. But don't forget your travel and accommodation costs. This option can work well for couples with families from different locations, since a midpoint can make it easier for everyone to attend. It's worth considering the logistics before going for this option. Do you need to get any special permissions? Which is the best season for the location of your choice? Will you make it a several-day event if people are traveling far?

WHO?

It's important to know how many guests you will be inviting and if a venue can accommodate them all. Will the same number be at the ceremony and reception? Will you have additional guests for the evening? Will guests need to drive or get taxis between locations, or will you offer a bus service? Will guests need to stay overnight? Is it accessible to anyone with mobility issues? Is there a minimum number of guests the venue requires?

GENERAL TIPS AND QUESTIONS

- Are there good places to take photos?
- Are there rules about candles or confetti?
- Is there enough parking?
- Does the venue have an events manager?
- Consider the time of year. Do you want particular flowers or empty fields to be in your wedding photos?
- Can your guests stay at the location?
- Are there different packages available? Is the price calculated per head, per room rental, or is there a minimum spend?
- What are the bar options? Can you supply your own drinks? Is there a corkage fee?
- Are there noise restrictions? Does the DJ/band need to be finished by a certain time?
- Can you set up a day in advance?
- Does the venue provide all the tableware and do you like what they provide?
- Can you choose your own suppliers (caterer, florist, etc.)?
- Do you have a backup plan for bad weather if you're planning to be outdoors?
- Do you need special permissions for your ceremony or reception venue?
- Will you need to take out extra insurance?
- What are the staff numbers on the day?
- Get everything confirmed in writing.

CHOOSING A CATERER

YOU SHOULD HAVE ALREADY FINALIZED THE LOCATION, date, and time for your wedding. Now you need to consider the following before you embark on choosing a caterer too…

"After a good dinner one can forgive anybody, even one's own relations." -Oscar Wilde

Check with your venue

Your venue may have requirements on the caterer you use. If they have their own on-site kitchen they might require that you use their chef. When looking at venues it is important to find this out and check that you are happy with their food before booking that venue.

• Can you supply your own drinks, and, if so, what is the corkage fee?

• Is there a minimum or maximum head count?

• If they do not have requirements on which caterer you use, do they have recommendations?

Questions to ask

- Who will oversee the catering staff? How many members of staff will be serving the food?
- What can they offer for vegetarians, anyone with special dietary requirements, and children?
- What is the caterer's level or experience? Do they specialize in any one dish?
- Is there a menu tasting session and who pays for it—the couple or the caterer?
- What is the payment schedule? Is there a deposit or holding fee? What is their refund or cancellation fee?
- Does the caterer have a food standards/hygiene license and a license to serve alcohol?
- Is the food fresh or frozen?
- Do they charge extra for tea and coffee?
- Does the caterer lay out the table settings or does the venue?

Before you meet

It's important to know the basics of what you're expecting before meeting with any potential caterers. Ask yourself...

- Will the food be served buffet style, tray passed, or silver service?
- How many courses will be served?
- Do you also need to supply food for the photographer, florist, DJ/musicians, etc.? Factor this into your head count.
- What is your budget? How important of a role will the food and beverages have at your wedding?

Top tip

Your caterer may also supply wedding cakes. Ask if you receive a discount if you order your cake through them instead of a bakery.

CHOOSING A PHOTOGRAPHER

YOU'LL BE LOOKING AT PHOTOS OF YOUR WEDDING DAY for many years to come, so it's important to make sure your day is captured just as you want it to be.

Choosing a photographer and/or videographer for your wedding is a decision that requires a lot of consideration. Here are tips to help you choose the right person to photograph your wedding.
• Speak to friends to see if you can get good recommendations.
• See if your venue has a list of trusted photographers/videographers.

• Do research online and check local listings in your area or in the area where the wedding will be. Some photographers charge for travel costs.
• A photographer's website can give you clues to what they're like. Have they invested lots of time and money in their website? Is it easy to navigate?
• Set up interviews and give them an idea of what you envision for the day.
• If your wedding is in dark light conditions or an unusual setting then ask a photographer to show you work that they have done that is similar.
• Ask about packages and don't be afraid to negotiate.
• Will the photographer have an assistant on the day?
• Will the photographer keep the copyright? Are they willing to give you any photos on a disc? When will you get your photos and wedding album?
• Will the photographer upload photos to their website for guests to view and buy?
• How much retouching work will the photographer do to the images?

Expert Tips

1 Choose a style of photography that you like, then research photographers with that style.

2 If you find a photographer you like, check if they have any feedback on social media sites, blogs, etc. See how they've responded to comments they've received.

3 Photographers often show a sample wedding portfolio of all their best shots, but you really want to see at least one or two complete weddings they've done.

4 It's important to meet them face-to-face to make sure your personalities fit. You should feel comfortable around them.

5 Once you've chosen a photographer, he or she will ask you to sign a contract. Find out if there is a cancellation fee and if you need to pay a deposit.

Having a mixture of black-and-white and color photographs gives you plenty of options.

"Nothing is ever really lost to us as long as we remember it."
-L. M. Montgomery

PHOTO LIST

THE PHOTOGRAPHER wants to make sure he or she captures every special moment and everyone in the photo groupings, so it's important to provide a comprehensive list.

By creating a list, you can help allocate a slot for official photos to be taken during the day. You can also allow time for bride and groom portraits to be done. If there's a photo you've seen and really like then you can ask your photographer to try and re-create it. Do a little bit of research.

Photographers are often happy to visit the venue with you and your groom before the big day. This is the perfect opportunity for the photographer and couple to think about what types of photo they want on the day and to find any interesting angles or backdrops that can be incorporated into the photography on the day of the wedding.

The possibilities are endless, so make sure you and your photographer stick to the time allocated for making the portraits. If not, your guests and caterers will be wondering where you are. A good wedding photographer will make the couple feel at ease, and the photos will look natural and will show the couple relaxed and having fun.

BEFORE THE CEREMONY

- Bride and bridesmaids getting ready
- Bride in her dress
- Bouquets and boutonnieres
- Bride with mother/father/both parents
- Bride with maid of honor/flower girl/all bridesmaids
- Bride's parents
- Any other members of the bridal party or groom getting ready

AT THE CEREMONY

- Guests arriving at the venue
- Groom and best man at the altar
- Ushers escorting guests
- Groom with ushers
- Whole venue with guests seated
- Bride and father getting out of the wedding car and going into the venue
- Musicians
- Flower girl and bridesmaids walking up the aisle
- Bride and father walking up the aisle
- Exchanging of the rings
- Bride and groom kissing
- Posed shot of signing the marriage license (it is illegal to photograph the actual signing in some countries)
- Bride and groom walking down the aisle at the end of the ceremony
- Bride and groom getting into the wedding car

BEFORE THE RECEPTION

- Bride and groom with entire wedding party and guests
- Bride with her bouquet
- Bride and maid of honor/ flower girl/all bridesmaids
- Groom
- Groom and best man/ ushers
- Bride and groom with all attendants
- Bride/groom with bride's parents
- Bride/groom with groom's parents
- Bride/groom with both mothers
- Bride/groom with both fathers
- Bride/groom with both sets of parents
- Groom with his mother
- Bride and groom with groom's parents
- Bride and groom with bride's parents
- Bride and groom with both sets of parents
- Bride and groom with both fathers
- Bride and groom with both mothers
- Bride/groom with grandparents
- Bride/groom with siblings

AT THE RECEPTION

- Guests mingling
- Bride and groom arriving
- Bride and groom going into the reception
- Group shots of guests
- Entertainers and musicians
- Room shot
- Table shots
- Table names and seating plan
- Close-ups of centerpieces and favors
- Cake
- Gift table
- Receiving line
- Bride and groom cutting the cake
- Bride and groom toasting each other
- Speeches
- Bride and groom's first dance
- Groom and mother dancing
- Bride and father dancing
- Bride throwing bouquet
- Guest catching bouquet
- Bride and groom getting into the car
- Rear of car as it drives off

BRIDE AND GROOM PORTRAITS

If there is somewhere near the venue that is important to the couple, such as a park or a body of water, then the photographer and couple can disappear for an hour while the guests drink champagne and eat appetizers.

Shots that are commonly set up for bride and groom are:

- The bride in the foreground with the groom in the distance
- The bride and groom underneath an archway
- The bride and groom in front of the church or town hall
- The groom picking up the bride
- The groom with his arms around the bride's waist
- The bride on her own
- The groom on his own
- The bouquet in the foreground and in focus with the bride and groom in the background.

"If I had a *flower* for every time I thought of you... I could walk through my garden forever."
-Alfred, Lord Tennyson

CHOOSING YOUR BRIDAL PARTY

PEOPLE OFTEN HAVE CERTAIN EXPECTATIONS when it comes to choosing attendants for a bridal party. For example, a best friend or sibling might expect to be chosen. You need to think, however, about who is right for the job. Consider the list on the next page before you make your final choices.

TRADITIONS

Traditionally, best friends or siblings are chosen to be maid of honor and best man. Nieces, nephews, or children of close friends are often asked to be a flower girl or a ring bearer. It's important to decide whether the child is old enough to take on the responsibility, since it's a lot of pressure to put on a youngster. Bridesmaids and groomsmen are usually good friends or relatives. You need to create a bridal party that is helpful, enthusiastic, and that will fulfill specific roles on the day.

MODERN NAMES

Today, if a best friend is of the opposite sex he or she can still be included in the bridal party. A groom might have a groomswoman as an usher or even as his best man.

OTHER ROLES

If you're unable to fit a friend or family member into your bridal party then think about other ways in which they can be involved. A cousin might be happy to sing a song or play a piece of music, an aunt might be willing and able to make your cake, and a good friend could do a reading. There's often much to get done that others would be happy to help with.

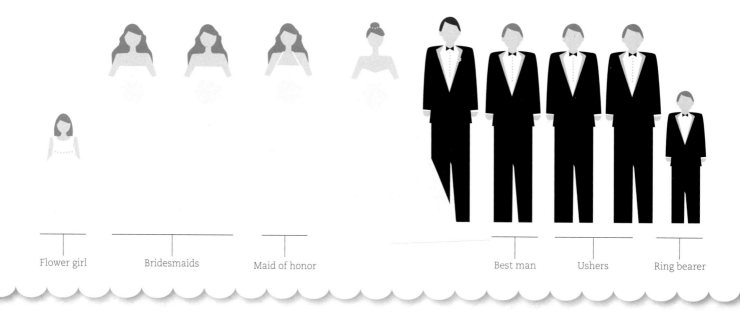

Flower girl   Bridesmaids   Maid of honor   Best man   Ushers   Ring bearer

POINTS TO CONSIDER

1 Don't be afraid to take your time thinking about your selection. Each person needs to be right for a chosen role. Let your engagement sink in before making any decisions.

2 Think about your budget. You might have 10 really good friends, but if you're planning on paying for the bridesmaids' dresses you might blow your budget if you include them all.

3 What's your venue like? Would it look crowded or over the top to have a large bridal party escort you down the aisle or stand at the front during the ceremony? Trying to coordinate so many people can often be difficult and might result in more stress than helping hands.

4 Think about how the bridesmaids and ushers will get along as a group. You don't want to be dealing with unnecessary drama during your wedding day or in the run-up to it.

5 Who can you really count on? Each member of your bridal party needs to be able to fulfill a specific role. Your younger sister might be your sister, but if she can't be relied on or has very different taste from you then she might not be the best choice for your maid of honor. If the groom's best friend is terribly shy, will it be too much to expect him to make a best man's speech in front of all your guests?

6 Who is actually able to help you? If your bridesmaid is pregnant or has children then even though she might want to help, she may not be able to be there as much as someone else. The same goes for any friend who has a busy schedule or who doesn't live nearby. If you want help with making things for your wedding or on shopping excursions then it is worth considering these points.

7 Don't let anyone put pressure on your choices (including the future mothers-in-law!). If you don't want to have your niece or nephew as a flower girl or ring bearer then be honest.

8 Just because you were a bridesmaid for someone doesn't mean you have to return the favor. Remember that a true friend will always respect your decision. There's nothing worse than a friend who expects to be picked for a role and then gets upset if someone else is chosen.

MAID OF HONOR'S DUTIES

THE MAID OF HONOR IS THERE TO ASSIST the bride with any requests or help she might need, and to support the bride through what can, at times, be a stressful period. She might be called upon to do anything, from addressing invitations to picking up the flowers from the florist.

The maid of honor
usually plays a bigger role in the wedding planning than the best man does, simply because it is usual for the bride to do more of the wedding planning than the groom.

The maid of honor may therefore find herself addressing invitations and going with the bride to test out hairstyles and makeup, while the best man takes more of a backseat until the bachelor party is being planned. Both people's roles are fundamental to the big day though.

PRE-WEDDING DUTIES

• To nod enthusiastically and speak encouragingly during any wedding conversations. She should be honest, but always supportive, about the bride's choices.

• To collect money from the bridesmaids to purchase a gift for the bride. This might be something to help her fulfill one aspect of the "Something old, something new, something borrowed, something blue" tradition.

• To help the bride find her wedding gown; go to all the trying-on outings, and attend every dress fitting with the bride once she's found the perfect dress.

• To make suggestions for, and help the bride choose, the bridesmaid dresses. Liaise with the other bridesmaids to ensure they can make any shopping expeditions and attend their fittings.

• To arrange certain parties in honor of the bride; host a bridal shower for the bride, and, of course, organize the bachelorette party. If there are other bridesmaids, the maid of honor may be able to delegate some of these planning responsibilities, from sending out the shower or party invitations to helping the bride-to-be shop for her outfits for both events.

ON THE DAY

• To be supportive and deflect any problems away from the bride that may arise during the day. The maid of honor will need to make sure everything runs on schedule, and make sure the bride eats something amid the flurry of the day... as well as ensuring that there's a bottle of champagne ready for popping once she's ready and in her dress.

• To help the bride get into her dress, buttoning up each and every tiny pearl fastening,

• To hold the bride's bouquet during the ceremony.

• To help adjust the bride's veil and dress as she stands and sits throughout the ceremony and throughout the day.

• To act as a witness and sign the marriage license along with the best man.

• To help the bride with her dress, if needed, when she visits the bathroom.

• To play hostess during the reception, sharing such jobs with the best man as directing guests to sign the guest book and showing them where to put any gifts.

• To help round up the appropriate people for each group photograph.

• To toast the happy couple. The maid of honor may also be asked to give a speech, but isn't required to do so.

• To dance with the best man at the appropriate time during the first dance.

• To help the best man decorate the car in which the couple will be traveling before they set off, adding the female touch.

POST-WEDDING

• To help the bride out of her dress and into her travel clothes, if she is leaving for her honeymoon that night.

• To take the bride's dress to be professionally cleaned and properly stored while the bride is on her honeymoon.

Global facts

Around the world, bridesmaids have different meanings in different cultures and religions.

The Western tradition is believed to have descended from a Roman law requiring 10 witnesses at a wedding dressed identically to the bride and groom. This was believed to outwit any evil spirits in attendance, so that they wouldn't know who was getting married.

This may have carried over into modern expressions such as "Always a bridesmaid, never a bride" because it was believed that the repeated exposure to the bad spirits had a cumulative unlucky effect on the bridesmaid—meaning she would never get married herself.

BEST MAN'S DUTIES

THE SPEECH AND BACHELOR PARTY are just two of the many responsibilities that a best man takes on when he agrees to take the job. Read below to find out what else is traditionally expected of this important role.

PRE-WEDDING

• Collect money from the members of the groom's party to purchase a gift for the groom.

• Help the groom choose the suit or tuxedo for him and the groomsmen, and to liaise with the groomsmen to ensure the correct sizes are ordered for everyone.

• Responsibly organize the bachelor party—the most publicized role of the best man. Depending on whether the bachelorette and bachelor parties are joint or separate will dictate whether the best man needs to liaise with the maid of honor.

ON THE DAY

• Get the groom to the church on time (and in one piece).

• Help the groom get ready, helping him with his cuff links, tie, and even his shoelaces, if necessary...

• Look after the rings if there is no ring bearer.

• Act as a witness and sign the marriage license, along with the maid of honor.

• Play host during the reception, along with the maid of honor.

• Help round up the appropriate people for each group photograph.

• Take charge of collecting and keeping safe any gifts and cards for the happy couple.

• Ensure that all vendors and suppliers—from the gardener who clears up the confetti to the band at the reception—who need to be paid on the day receive payment and tips.

• Make a speech—be it humorous or touching, or both—and toast the happy couple.

• Dance with the maid of honor at the appropriate time during the newlyweds' first dance.

• Decorate the car with the necessary "Just Married" sign and tin cans trailing from the back bumper.

POST-WEDDING

• Arrange transportation for or drive the newlyweds himself off into the sunset... to begin their honeymoon.

• Return the groom's and groomsmens' tuxedos to the rental store soon after the wedding, if appropriate.

AROUND THE WORLD

In different places around the world the best man at a wedding has different meanings and expectations. In India and Ukraine, for instance, the "best man" guards the bride during the wedding celebration and, if she is "kidnapped" under his watch, must perform an embarrassing skit for her return. In Uganda, the best man is an adviser and confidante who offers advice and counsel to guide the couple through their married life.

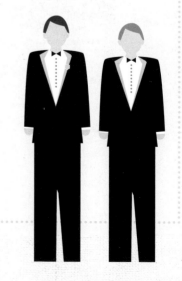

MUSIC AND ENTERTAINMENT

MUSIC AND ENTERTAINERS help to create an ambience and special mood for your wedding day. Consider all of these points before making any bookings.

MUSIC FOR THE CEREMONY, COCKTAIL HOUR, AND WEDDING RECEPTION

Think about how you envision your wedding day. Do you see music as a key element or as playing a small part? What KIND of music would you like for the bride's entrance and the couple's exit from the ceremony? Do you want something traditional or more modern? Carefully work through all of your options before making any decisions.

• First, do you want live music or are you happy to have prerecorded music? If you're playing a song that isn't live, do you need to pay to use the song?
• Do you want music to be played as the guests arrive?

Global Weddings

CERTAIN musical instruments play a key part in weddings around the world. In India, an oboe ("shehnai"), a wind instrument ("nadaswaram"), and/or drums are often played.

• Would you like any music during the signing of the marriage license?
• Is it possible to play the song you want in the ceremony location? If you're getting wed in a nonreligious venue then you may not be able to use religious songs.
• If you're hiring a string quartet or a pianist, are they willing to play for the ceremony, the cocktail hour, and the reception? Can you get a discount if they play at more than one part of your day?
• Is there a particular piece of music that is important to you and your partner? Do you want it played as the bride walks down the aisle, when the couple walks down the aisle at the end of the ceremony, or do you want to save it for your first dance?

BAND AND/OR DJ?

Whether you decide to hire a band or a DJ for your evening music, it's worth asking the following questions...
• What's your budget?
• Do you want a band and a DJ or just one of them?
• Do you want a tribute band or is there a particular genre you're after?
• Does the band/DJ have a fixed set list or can you ask for special requests?
• Does the band need a stage? If so, does your venue have one? Is there enough space for a band to play?
• Does your venue have any restrictions on noise levels or types of music?
• Is there somewhere for the band to set up while the wedding reception is taking place? How will you make the changeover from your reception meal to the evening's dancing?
• Can you see the band/DJ perform before your wedding? Do they have a few demos on their website?

MEETING WITH ARTISTS

Once you've worked out exactly what you want, start to arrange meetings with a selection of the performers and entertainers that you like. Double-check their availability and price before meeting with them. Come prepared to your interviews and ask all of the following questions:

• How many hours does the price include? Do you charge overtime? Do you take breaks? If so, how long are they?

• What's your playlist and can we and/or the guests make special requests? Can we submit a "Do Not Play" list?

• What is your cancellation policy?

• Will you be doing more than one event on the day?

• What kind of equipment do you use? Do you bring backup equipment to the wedding? Do you bring your own lights? Do you have a wireless microphone?

• What do you normally wear to the wedding? Can we make wardrobe requests?

• What is your policy on drinking? You don't want a DJ who "needs a few drinks" to loosen him up before he plays.

• What's your experience?

• Do you belong to any professional associations or trade groups?

• What makes you different from your competitors?

• How do you fill the dance floor if it's suddenly become empty?

• Can we sign a contract before paying?

• May we speak to your references?

• Do you make announcements as the MC for the night? If so, what would you say your style of doing so is?

• What happens if you can't perform on the night?

ALTERNATIVE ENTERTAINMENT

Couples might choose a magician, a children's entertainer, a bouncy castle, a photo booth, a video message booth, an ice-cream van, singing waiters, a caricaturist, ballet dancers, performance artists, a chocolate fountain, look-alikes, fireworks, or even a casino! Think about how important alternative entertainment is for your day. For some couples it will add to their theme and leave lasting memories for them and for their guests.

Ideas for your first dance

As with all aspects of a wedding, music and dances are down to personal choice. If you've decided you want to have a first dance then there are a few things to consider...

Music genres and dance styles Is there a particular type of music that you both like? Is there a dance style you want to use; fox-trot, salsa, rumba, waltz, swing, shuffle, sway, or anything goes!

Dance classes Do you want to attend dance classes together in preparation for your first dance?

"Our song" Was there a song playing when you first met? Is there a band/musician you both particularly love?

Choosing a florist

FLOWERS ARE INTEGRAL to the atmosphere of your wedding. Selecting the right florist is key to getting a major part of your wedding day the way you want it.

The most important thing is to find a florist who understands exactly what you want and someone who can interpret your vision and with whom you can work. The best way to find a florist is to go by recommendations from friends and from wedding websites and magazines. Check local directories for florists near to the venue. Look online and at wedding magazines to get inspiration for colors and types of flowers.

Meet with your florist to run through the questions below and to show them a mood board. If you're happy with the florist, then book them right away. Florists (especially good ones) tend to get booked up in advance. You won't need to meet with the florist again until a few months before your wedding, when you'll make final decisions on flowers.

THIS BEAUTIFUL BOUQUET is made up of roses, spray roses, astilbe, cineraria, stock, and cotinus.

• What flowers and greenery will be in season when I get married?
• Do you have any ideas that will fit with my wedding theme?

• Can you show me photos and testimonials from previous weddings?
• Have you provided flowers for the venue before?
• How many weddings do you do a year?
• If my wedding falls in a busy period (Mother's Day, Valentine's, etc.) are there limits to what I can choose?

• Can you preserve my bouquet?
• Can you suggest cheaper flowers to help with the overall cost? Or can I share flowers with someone else who is getting married at the venue on the same day?
• Do you deliver the flowers to my home or to the venue?
• When do I pay the deposit?
• Ask for an itemized quotation.

Bouquet types

NOSEGAY This design is a small and compact collection of flowers cut to the same length. The handle is wrapped in ribbon.

HAND-TIED Another classic bouquet, ideal for more informal weddings, since it has a looser look than the other bouquet types.

POSY This is a classic shape for a bridal bouquet. It's not too big and has a round shape. Ribbon is wrapped around a handle.

POMPANDER A flower covered ball, with a ribbon handle. The flower girl can carry a smaller version of the bride's pompander.

A COMPOSITE bouquet is made up of petals or buds wired together on a single stem.

ROUND This bouquet is a tighter and more formal version of the hand-tied bouquet. The stems are wrapped in ribbon.

A TEAR-DROP or arm bouquet is hand-tied with raffia or string. The flowers are close together and cascade downward.

PINK AND RED FLOWERS

Flowers in these colors include: roses, snapdragons, gerbera, tulips, dahlias, hydrangeas, orchids, carnations, cockscomb, and lisianthus.

PURPLE FLOWERS

The spectrum of purple flowers goes from light to dark. Choose from stock, chrysanthemums, orchids, scabiosa, hydrangeas, dahlias, lisianthus, and veronica.

YELLOW FLOWERS

You can have any of the following flowers in this color range: gerbera, roses, chrysanthemums, orchids, mimosa, lilies, tulips, daffodils, sunflowers, and ranunculus.

BLUE FLOWERS

Beautiful blue flowers include hydrangeas, thistle, anemomes, brodea, hyacinth, delphiniums, irises, and cornflowers.

ORANGE FLOWERS

Select from a wide range of orange flowers: roses, calla lilies, orchids, tulips, ranunculus, dahlias, gerberas, protea, carnations, and lilies.

WHITE FLOWERS

The range is broad—you can have calla lilies, chamomile, ornithogalum, roses, tulips, carnations, gerberas, stock, peonies, hydrangeas, and lilies.

GREEN FLOWERS

Choose from hydrangeas, alchemilla, guelder rose, green roses, anthuriums, orchids, and chrysanthemums. Use lots of greenery in your bouquet.

PEACH FLOWERS

Lovely and light, peach flowers include: roses, spray roses, ranunculus, gerbera, tulips, peonies, astilbe, carnations, and lilies.

DRESS SHAPES

FOR MANY BRIDES, THE DRESS is one of the most important parts of the day. Try on different shapes and styles—something you didn't have in mind might surprise you. Always try sitting and dancing in a dress to make sure it is comfortable.

A-Line

An a-line dress can help to balance out larger busts, drawing the eye down. It can also work well for pear-shaped women, helping to disguise the hips.

Fishtail

Fitted all the way down with a flare out at the knee, fishtail dresses can be very constricting. Good for those with a balanced shape, such as an hourglass.

Trumpet

Similar to a fishtail, but with a flare off from the thigh. Trumpet shaped dresses are a bit easier to move in than fishtail dresses are.

Empire

Good for apple-shaped bodies, an empire line sits just below the bust, drawing the eye up and away from the tummy. Also good for shorter brides, elongating the body. Avoid if you are top-heavy.

Ballgown

One of the most traditional wedding gown shapes. The ballgown suits almost every shape, except petite brides, who may look swamped.

Sheath

Best for slim brides with straight shapes. The sheath can also work well for hourglass shapes, if the dress has a defined waist, and for petite brides with small frames.

NECKLINE DECODER

ONCE YOU'VE DECIDED ON A DRESS SHAPE, the next thing to choose is which neckline you'd like. The decision might go hand-in-hand if you're choosing from ready-made designs, but most dress shapes come in a variety of neckline options.

Sweetheart

Shaped like the top half of a heart, this neckline works well for large-busted brides, showing off their decolletage.

Straight

Showcase your collar bones and shoulders with this strapless option. Works well on petite brides.

V-neck

A V-neck will lengthen the neck and draw attention away from the bust. Best on medium-busted brides.

Asymmetric

Best for slimmer brides and those with long necks. Be careful if you have a large bust or broad shoulders.

Halter neck

A halter neck works well to break up broad shoulders. Be careful if you have bulky upper arms or a large bust.

Off the Shoulder

Perfect for pear-shaped and well-endowed brides. Best avoided with broad shoulders.

Queen Anne

Good for brides looking for a bit of coverage or petite brides. Elongates and opens up the neck.

Boat Neck

Great to balance out wide hips, this also works well with a small chest. Be careful if you have broad shoulders.

Square

Good for round faces, narrow shoulders, and pear shapes. Best avoided if you have a square face shape.

Cowl

A cowl neck can be universally flattering, just be careful with the weight of the fabric and the shape of the armhole.

TRAIN LENGTH

THE LENGTH OF THE TRAIN is traditionally dictated by the formality of the wedding; the more formal the wedding, the longer the train. Today, most brides pick the length solely on preference. You can also choose not to have a train at all.

Watteau

A watteau train is a single, separate panel that attaches at the top of the dress near the shoulders. It can be any length and works well with sheath-style dresses.

Royal

Trailing a yard or more behind you, a royal-length train is for the most formal of weddings. It will require a lot of attention from your bridesmaids.

Cathedral

A cathedral length train extends more than 22in (56cm) behind a dress and is for formal weddings. It can require a lot of attention for photos and will probably need to be bustled for the reception.

Sweep

Also called a brush train, this length just "brushes" the ground behind your dress, usually about 6in (15cm) beyond the hem. Aside from no train at all, the sweep train is the easiest to wear and is appropriate for most ceremonies.

Chapel

Extending about 12-18in (30-46cm) behind you, the chapel length is the most popular train. It can add a touch of elegance without too much weight.

VEIL LENGTH

THE TRADITION OF THE VEIL dates back to Roman times, when brides wore veils to help ward off evil spirits. It also helped protect the bride and groom from seeing one another before the ceremony, considered a form of bad luck.

Construction

Veils are made of two parts. One part sits stationary on the head, while the other drapes over the bride's face. The length of a veil traditionally corresponds to the formality of the ceremony with the longest, cathedral length, only being used in the most formal of weddings.

Birdcage

Birdcage veils do not extend past the chin and resemble more of a fascinator. If your gown has a higher neckline, or is vintage, this can work well.

Shoulder

Also called blusher length. For less formal ceremonies. Can work well if you have detail on the bodice of your dress you'd like to showcase.

Elbow

Suits a ballgown dress well since it stops at the point where the full skirt begins. It falls just over the shoulders, providing a bit of coverage.

Fingertip

Perhaps the most popular length, fingertip veils suit almost any dress shape, but be careful with the length if your dress has a train.

Floor length

A floor length veil should match the length of the front of your dress. Because of its length, it can change the look of the body's silhouette.

Chapel

A chapel length veil brushes the floor behind you and can be worn as an alternative to a train. The veil can be removed before the reception, and no bustling is required, as with a train.

Cathedral

A cathedral length veil extends beyond the length of a train behind you and gives a very formal and dramatic appearance.

WEDDING CAKE IDEAS

THE WEDDING CAKE is a focal point of your special day. Choose one that's in keeping with your theme and look. Make sure it's large enough to allow for a slice per guest.

TIERED CAKE

Three tiers are seen as the classic wedding cake. The top tier is often frozen and eaten on the couple's first wedding anniversary. The middle tier is portioned out for the guests to take home and the bottom tier is eaten at the wedding.

WHITE ICING

White icing on wedding cakes first appeared in Victorian times. The wedding cake was traditionally referred to as the bride's cake. The white icing echoed the bride's white dress. White icing also showed the affluence of a family, since the ingredients to make the icing were hard to come by. White icing was made from the most refined sugar, which was incredibly expensive.

FAKE CAKES

At some weddings only the top tier is edible. This is for the couple to eat and the rest is for show!

PRETTY PEARLS made from icing are a perfect cake covering for a blush or a metropolitan cake.

"*Life* is the flower
for which *love* is
the honey."
~ *Victor Hugo*

CUTTING THE CAKE

Couples often cut the cake together as a symbol that they are now joined together in matrimony. It's a classic wedding photo that many couples have in their album.

CAKE TOPPERS

Couples can choose from a range of things to top their cake. Some choose a bride and groom that are made to look like the couple. The topper can be edible, or it can be ceramic or plastic. The topper needs to suit the wedding theme. It's up to the bride and groom to choose. Cakes can also be adorned with fresh flowers or flowers made from icing.

TYPES OF DECORATIONS

Metallic cakes Iced with metallic edible glitter... think art deco.

White-on-white Adorned with pearls or flowers made from icing.

A lacy number The icing is made to look like lace.

Rosette cakes Cakes completely covered in roses made from icing.

Painted wedding cake The icing is used to make a piece of art.

Geometric cakes The icing creates geometric patterns.

Ruffled cakes The icing forms a ruffle effect.

Naked cakes There isn't any traditional icing on the outside.

Pure buttercream The cake is covered in buttercream frosting.

Natural A traditional cake is covered in real flowers.

HOW MANY TIERS?

USE THIS GUIDE to work out how many tiers you will need on your cake to feed all your guests.

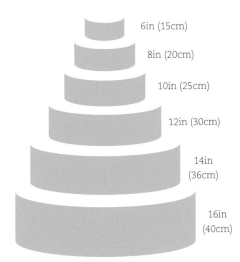

6in (15cm)
8in (20cm)
10in (25cm)
12in (30cm)
14in (36cm)
16in (40cm)

THIS ROUND CAKE provides 318 pieces that are 1 x 2in (2.5 x 5cm) in size. From top to bottom the tiers allow 10, 28, 42, 56, 82, and 100 pieces.

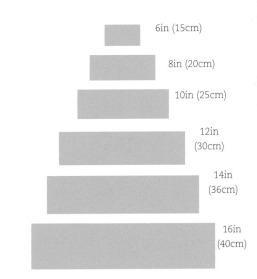

6in (15cm)
8in (20cm)
10in (25cm)
12in (30cm)
14in (36cm)
16in (40cm)

THIS SQUARE CAKE provides 398 pieces that are 1 x 2in (2.5 x 5cm) in size. From top to bottom the tiers allow 18, 32, 50, 72, 98, and 128 pieces.

PLANNING A HONEYMOON

It's the beginning of the rest of your life together,

and what better way to start than with a romantic trip away.

"Paradise is always where love dwells."

– Johann Paul Friedrich Richter

TYPE OF HONEYMOON

Going "all-inclusive" will generally get you the most for your money, but the resort vacation isn't for everyone. Many couples choose to make the most of the special occasion and vacation time to travel through far-away lands. Others prefer to visit a favorite spot closer to home, do a city break, or rent a car for a long-dreamed-about road trip. Whatever you decide, decide together.

WHEN TO GO

Traditionally, honeymooners leave right after the wedding. If you are one of these couples, you are most likely to want to book a relaxing break now that you've escaped the crowds of family and friends. However, many couples wait a few months to go on their honeymoon, which can have other benefits—work and vacation time reasons, for the desired weather, or to get better deals. Some couples choose to do a mini-moon for a few days right after the wedding, saving their big honeymoon for a few months later.

WHAT TO DO

It may sound silly to suggest coming up with a list of goals for your honeymoon. But, thinking about what you want to do while you're there will help you decide what type of honeymoon you actually want. Sitting and relaxing on a beach, for example, is all very good, but how long would you last before getting bored? Many destinations offer something for everyone—relaxing opportunities alongside outings and activities.

HOW TO BOOK

You might want to consider using a travel agent, who can save you a lot of time and stress by researching options for you based on your criteria. They also have inside knowledge about deals and can make you a personalized package. However, they usually charge a commission, and you don't receive online prices, which are often cheaper. You need to weigh cost against stress.

What name should the bride use for the honeymoon booking?

If applying for new passport in your married name, confirm how far in advance this can be done. Also, make sure the new passport is valid before the old one is canceled. This can be an issue for those traveling to a destination wedding. Tickets and reservations should be made in the name listed on the valid passport you will use.

Do you need a visa?

Apply for any visas with plenty of time to spare. Depending on where you are traveling, the visa could take months to be granted and your passport returned to you.

Do you need vaccinations or anti-malarial tablets?

Check what vaccinations or tablets you might need to have ahead of your trip and how far in advance they need to be given. Also, check whether you need a vaccination passport, for example, for yellow fever.

SURPRISE!

If it's the groom's task to plan the honeymoon as a surprise for the bride, make sure you choose somewhere that she's always wanted to go. Also, give her enough information on what to pack for the climate and any activities.

Practicalities

Buy travel insurance

Check that your policy covers you for the appropriate medical care, including accidents that are a result of any planned activities, such as skiing or water sports.

Think ahead

Check ahead about any specific restaurants, day trips, or spa treatments you want to do, and whether you should book in advance. You don't want to get there and find you miss out simply because they're fully booked.

Bridal shower

TRADITIONAL DOWRY PRACTICES may have been a precursor to modern bridal showers. Guests "showered" the bride with gifts to help her set up her new home comfortably. Today, shower gifts can be anything from lingerie to contributions toward the honeymoon fund.

TRADITION BEHIND A BRIDAL SHOWER

Bridal showers are traditionally held about two months before the wedding. They are hosted by bridesmaids or friends of the bride. You should not invite anyone to the shower who hasn't been invited to the actual wedding (except in the case of an office shower). Invitations should only be sent to the guests four to six weeks in advance. The shower allows the bride to get used to being the center of attention and it shows support for the bride and the marriage. There are many traditions surrounding a bridal shower. Here's a small selection:

• The groom shows up partway through the shower with a bouquet of fresh flowers for the bride. This gives guests who may not have met the groom the opportunity to do so before the wedding day.

• The maid of honor creates a faux bouquet out of all the ribbons and bows tied onto the presents. The bride then uses this as a practice bouquet during the wedding rehearsal.

• The bride might receive her something old, something new, something borrowed, and something blue at the bridal shower. These are then checked off the list before the big day.

WHAT HAPPENS AT A BRIDAL SHOWER

The bride and the host welcome all the guests as they arrive. Snacks and drinks are served and games are often played. It's a time for guests and relatives to meet for the first time, or simply catch up. At some point during the shower, gifts are given for the bride to open.

GIFT LIST

As with a baby shower, presents are expected at a bridal shower. It's one of the main reasons for getting the bride and guests together. It's perfectly acceptable to have a bridal shower gift registry at your favorite store. Gift list information can be included on the bridal shower invitation.

BRIDAL SHOWER THEMES

Bridal showers can have a theme to make them more unusual and give them a focus. Here are a few suggestions:

• FLOWER POWER Each guest brings along a different type of flower (this can be decided beforehand or done at random). The flowers are used to make a bouquet that can feature at the shower and be taken home by the bride at the end.

• MEMORIES Guests write down a memory they have of the bride in the time that they've known her. They have to bring a present that links to that memory of the bride.

• FAVORITE THINGS The party is planned around a few of the bride's favorite things: her favorite color, flower, foods, etc.

• TEA PARTY For a classic feminine take, a traditional tea party might be just the thing. Ladies can wear hats and eat a traditional cream tea out on the lawn, weather permitting.

• SHOE BOX If the shower is being held farther afield, then each gift being brought for the bride needs to be able to fit inside a shoe box, so that the bride can easily transport everything back home.

• LOCATIONS The theme can be linked to a place, such as Paris. Think champagne and French food.

IDEAS FOR GAMES

• MAKE A WEDDING DRESS for the bride over her clothes. Use toilet paper, white printer paper, or even a couple of newspapers.

• GUESS WHAT'S INSIDE is a fun game to play that tests the knowledge of the guests. The bride hands around a large bag with items found around the house. The guests have to feel the bag to guess which items are inside.

• CREATE A SCRAPBOOK for the bride. Each guest needs to bring along photos, trinkets, and other things that remind them of the bride. Each guest then gets creative making a page. The book is then assembled and presented to the bride.

OFFICE BRIDAL SHOWER

If a bride can't afford to invite all of her colleagues from work, but would still like to celebrate with them, then an office bridal shower can be arranged. This could be at a restaurant or cocktail bar near the office.

Often, colleagues of the bride may want to buy a present even if they won't be at the wedding, so this is the perfect opportunity.

"When *love* is not **madness**
it is not *love*."
-Pedro Calderón de la Barca

GLOBAL BACHELOR AND BACHELORETTE CELEBRATIONS

IT'S TIME TO GET YOUR PARTY SHOES ON and celebrate in style. However you decide to mark the occasion, bachelor and bachelorette parties are all about having fun, and toasting the end of single life and the start of a new chapter.

TRADITION BEHIND THE EVENT

Bachelor and bachelorette parties are known for being rowdy occasions, but they can be classy too. It depends on the bride- or groom-to-be and the type of night or weekend that they would like. It's the responsibility of the best man and maid of honor to arrange the event. It's important when you select your best man and maid of honor that you think about whether they will be able to arrange the bachelor/bachelorette party and keep your wishes in mind. The tradition behind the party is that it's the bride and groom's last night of freedom before they commit to marriage.

COMBINED EVENTS

There are recent variations on the traditional event whereby both male and female guests are invited. Some couples decide to have their parties as a joint event. In Germany, couples invite their friends to a combined evening separate from the bachelor party called a "polterabend." Traditionally, at this event guests break pottery to make noise that wards off evil spirits from the wedding and marriage.

NAMES FOR THE CELEBRATION

This pre-wedding celebration of the groom has a slightly different name in the following countries...
• in Australia it's called a buck's night.
• in Canada, the UK, and Ireland the name used is a stag party, stag do, or stag night.
• in Germany a bachelor and a bachelorette party are both called a "Junggesellenabschied."
• in French-speaking regions it's called "enterrement de vie de garcon," which translates as "burial of life as a boy."

ARRANGING THE OCCASION

The bride or groom supplies a list of contact details for the guests, and the best man and maid of honor send out the invitations. Often, bachelor and bachelorette parties are expensive and can be a whole weekend or week away to another country, so give the guests plenty of notice, since they will need to keep the date free and save up for the occasion. If it's just a night out, then eight weeks' notice should be enough, but if the party is going to be abroad, then the guests will need to be informed six to eight months in advance.

BACHELORETTE PARTY

Celebrate in style Increasingly, destination parties have become popular. A getaway to a beach location or a city break are fitting. The bride might wear a fake veil and tiara, or be given a "bride to be" sash to wear. The party can be as simple or extravagant as you want it to be. Here are suggestions to get you thinking about what you would like...

Ideas for a bachelorette party

- Dance class
- Spa break
- City tour
- Cocktail-making lesson
- Boat trip
- Vintage photo shoot
- Retro night
- Treasure hunt
- Floral workshop
- Woodlands walk
- Make your own jewelry or pottery class
- Party bus
- Cabaret show
- Horseback riding
- Cooking class
- Recording a song
- Bike tour
- Life drawing
- Afternoon tea
- Theater trip
- Karaoke night
- Comedy club
- Fire engine tour
- Italian evening
- Chocolate workshop
- Amusement park
- Salsa evening

Helpful hint

AS A THANK YOU to your guests for coming to your event, treat them to a bottle of champagne or a round of cocktails.

BACHELOR PARTY

Time to party As with bachelorette parties, location bachelor parties are becoming more common. Trips to Las Vegas or Mexico aren't unheard of. If your budget doesn't stretch that far, have a themed party instead... rent a mini-casino or go out for a Mexican meal. Dress code can range from matching T-shirts to tuxedos to costumes.

Ideas for a bachelor party

- Driving quad bikes
- Zip lining
- Rage buggies
- River rafting
- Comedy night
- Themed pub crawl
- Festival trip
- Body zorbing
- Poker night
- Brewery tour
- Pizza making
- Go-karting
- Black ops lasertag
- Wine tasting
- City break
- Amusement park
- Surfing
- 4x4 off-road experience
- Paintball
- Jet skiing
- Mexican party
- Professional sports game
- Indoor skydiving

VOWS

AMID ALL THE FLOWERS AND CHAMPAGNE, décor- and dress-shopping, there is the serious part of the wedding that requires attention—THE VOWS. These are the bride and groom's declaration of their love for each other, and their solemn promise to love the other for the rest of their lives. The words you say in your vows are your verbal contract with one another, witnessed by family and friends. Some couples choose to say traditional, religious vows; others choose to write their own. Whatever route you decide to take with your vows, you should believe wholeheartedly in what they say, as you will be reciting them to the love of your life.

TYPES OF VOWS

For centuries, couples have recited the wedding vows of their religion or culture. Today, there are many options to choose from: there is the traditional option, the religious option, the nonreligious option, the civil option, the interfaith option… and, of course, the option to write your own wedding vows. Where you get married and who you choose to officiate will sometimes dictate your vows. If there are any restrictions your officiant will be able to supply you with your vow options and any approved variations for you to choose from. Either way, the officiant will ask to see the vows you have chosen before the day.

DIFFERENCES BETWEEN VOWS

Often, the reciting of vows signifies the moment when the bride and groom become husband and wife. What is said during religious vows varies depending on the religion. The point at which vows are recited during a ceremony also affects what is said. For example, at Jewish weddings, the vows are recited during the exchange of rings, but in other religions the rings are exchanged after the vows. If you are writing your own vows, it is worth considering when you want them to be said during the ceremony, since it may affect what you want to say. For example, you might want to acknowledge an exchange of the rings.

HOW TO RECITE THEM

There are different ways for couples to exchange their vows. Often, the choice is yours. Decide what you'll be most comfortable with, remembering that nerves might play a role.

1 The officiant can say a few lines at a time for you to repeat back.

2 The officiant can ask the vows as a question, and you will answer with "I do" or "I will."

3 You can both memorize the words you'd like to say.

4 You can both read your vows to each other.

HOW TO WRITE YOUR OWN VOWS

Traditional and religious vows tend to be very formal, and some people find it difficult to connect with the words, stumbling over the phrasing. Many couples therefore choose to write their own vows, or customize existing vows. Once you have an idea about what you would like to say, be sure to discuss it with your officiant to ensure they are happy for you to proceed and that the vows go with the type of ceremony you've chosen.

STRUCTURE

If you choose to write your own vows, will you write them together? Or will you write them separately so that the first time your fiancé hears them is on the day? If you write them together, do you want to say the same thing? If you write them separately, do you want them to follow a similar structure, such as beginning each sentence with "I promise to…" so that they mirror each other in structure and sentiment, if not in content?

CONTENT

Remember, your vows are just for you and your partner, and the words you say should be an expression of each of you and your relationship. You want your vows to be as personal as possible—after all, that's the benefit of writing your own. Some people find it easy to write their own vows; others find it difficult to put their feelings and emotion into words. Either way, remember that you have to speak them, so if you don't like speaking at length, make them concise. But the most important rule to remember when writing your own vows is that there are no rules for writing your vows. You can say whatever you want to say. Writing your own vows gives the bride and groom the opportunity to put their thoughts and feelings for each other into words.

Global fact

AT A TRADITIONAL Hindu wedding, the vows are said around a flame. They are called the seven steps, or "saptha padhi." The couple make seven promises to each other.

Speeches

YOU'VE SAID "I DO." You've signed the marriage license. You are now husband and wife. Following the photographs and the cocktails is the wedding reception—the traditional time for those much-planned and redrafted speeches.

"I... never could make a good impromptu speech without several hours to prepare it."

-Mark Twain

Who gives a speech?

Traditionally, the father of the bride opens the floor for the speeches, thanking the guests for attending and welcoming the groom's family into his own. Sometimes it is a solo few words; other times the mother of the bride likes to say something, too. Traditionally, the bride's parents host the wedding, and so it is right that they welcome the guests. But today, with many couples paying for their wedding themselves, this formality is often dropped.

Following the opening speech is the best man's speech, and then sometimes, the maid of honor will say a few words. The close relationships that these people share with the bride and groom automatically bring an intimacy to their words, and their speeches are often nostalgic and a little playful.

Next, the microphone is passed to the happy couple. Traditionally, the groom makes a speech, toasting his new wife and thanking the guests for sharing their special day. Some brides like to say a little something themselves, especially thanking the bridesmaids, as well as those friends and family who were so supportive and helpful during the wedding planning.

Other friends and family may also want to make a speech, but it is often best to limit the speeches to the traditional few.

When should the speeches occur?

Careful planning will have gone into every aspect of your wedding to ensure the day flows naturally, and the timing of the speeches should be no different. It is best to choose a time when everyone is already gathered together, which is why so many wedding speeches are given at some point during the dinner.

If any of the speakers are nervous it might be best to have the speeches before the dinner so that they can relax and enjoy themselves throughout the evening. Ultimately, though, it's completely up to you.

What should they say?

The best man's speech has become infamous for stealing the show with hilarity and anecdotes, but it doesn't have to follow this rule. A good speech is one that is delivered confidently, and so whoever gives the speech needs to feel comfortable and happy with what he is saying.

It is important to avoid any embarrassing situations, both in the content and in the delivery and response. It is equally important to be mindful of the truth behind the cliché, "Keep it short and sweet."

Tips for making a speech

- Don't wing it; plan it and practice saying it over and over again for a few weeks before the wedding.
- Write the speech with a beginning, middle, and end. Keep it concise, avoiding any long-winded stories and anecdotes, no matter how funny you think they are.
- Speak loudly and clearly. Don't rush through the words. Put marks on the paper, indicating pauses, to force you to slow down.
- Stay calm and stop to take a deep breath if you're feeling panicky or nervous. Have a glass of water on hand and pause for a drink if your mouth starts to dry out.
- Don't read line after line from your notes—you want it to come from the heart, so make eye contact and only use notes as a prompt. This is where the practice will help.
- Keep your alcohol intake to a minimum beforehand. Another reason to deliver the speeches early.

HEAD TABLE

THE HEAD TABLE, OR SWEETHEART TABLE, is where the bride and groom sit during the reception. It is the table that tends to have the most rules and traditions surrounding the placement of the wedding party guests.

Traditional seating plan

Traditionally, the parents of the couple as well as the best man and maid of honor are sat at the head table in a male-female alternating order.

| Maid of Honor | Groom's Father | Bride's Mother | GROOM |

THE HEAD TABLE

The head table is usually rectangular and is set at the front or side of the room, depending on the layout and venue. According to who you have at your wedding, their relation to you and one another, and how many people you need to seat at it, the seating arrangement will change.

In the UK, the head table encompasses the parents of the couple as well as the maid of honor and best man. However, in the US the head table consists of just the bridal party, shown above right. The parents of the couple each get their own "VIP" table to host consisting of guests of their choice, usually grandparents, godparents, or out-of-town relatives.

Here are some diagrams showing the traditional seating plan and some alternative options for the head table. The most traditional is shown large and other common alternatives are given on the next page. Really, you can do what suits you and your bridal party and family best. There is no point in sticking to tradition if it makes someone uncomfortable.

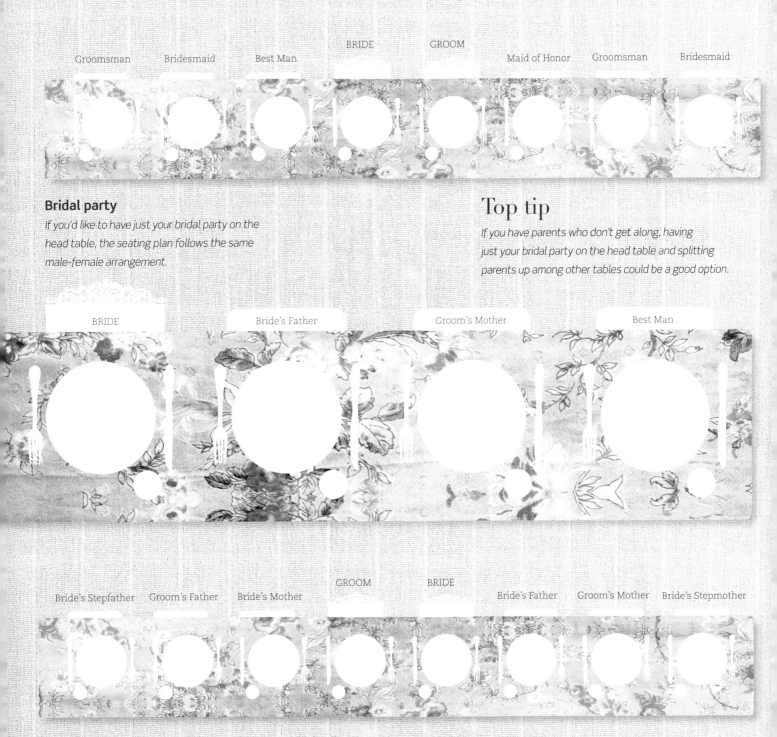

| Groomsman | Bridesmaid | Best Man | BRIDE | GROOM | Maid of Honor | Groomsman | Bridesmaid |

Bridal party

If you'd like to have just your bridal party on the head table, the seating plan follows the same male-female arrangement.

Top tip

If you have parents who don't get along, having just your bridal party on the head table and splitting parents up among other tables could be a good option.

| BRIDE | Bride's Father | Groom's Mother | Best Man |

| Bride's Stepfather | Groom's Father | Bride's Mother | GROOM | BRIDE | Bride's Father | Groom's Mother | Bride's Stepmother |

Remarried parents

If you have a non-traditional family, as many people do, you may have to do a bit of creative table arranging. To avoid making anyone uncomfortable, try to seat people where they won't have any conflict of interest.

Sweetheart table

A "sweetheart table" is when the bride and groom sit at a table alone together. If you have children or stepchildren you could also do a head table with just them.

SEATING PLAN

THE SEATING PLAN is an important part of planning your wedding. It ensures a smooth transition to dinner and helps make sure all your guests enjoy themselves.

Whether you have 40 or 200 guests, it's important to have a seating plan for your wedding reception meal. A successful seating plan will ensure that everyone you invite has someone to talk to and can turn a good evening into a great one. It also helps the evening run much more smoothly, since everyone will know exactly where to go. The seating plan requires a bit of thought by the couple, so it's a good idea to set aside some time to think and talk it through. There are no hard and fast rules in planning the seating, but there are a few things to consider. For example, you might want to decide whether to place guests next to people they know or mix them up so that they can mingle. You

Seat groups together or mix them up to give your guests a chance to mingle.

should also decide whether to mix the bride's and groom's guests. One solution is to aim for a bit of both—seat people in clusters of two to four—this way everyone has a few people they know to sit next to as well as the opportunity to meet others. Seat couples together and young children with their parents and make sure anyone attending the wedding alone is sitting near someone familiar. You can start planning the seating as soon as you have received most or all of your responses, but be prepared to be flexible in case of last-minute changes or cancellations.

HOW TO WORK IT OUT

There is software available online that can aid you in working out your seating arrangements, but if you like, you can just use a pen and paper and enlist the help of the humble sticky note. Cut a strip for each guest, using different colors for the bride's side, the groom's side, as well as different colors for friends and colleagues, if you wish. This will help you visualize where everyone will be seated. Contact the venue to find out what their tables are like and how many each one seats. You may even be given a choice at this point. Long, rectangular tables allow for more mixing, while round ones provide a more intimate setting. Draw the tables on a large piece of paper and start placing your guests in groups, filling each table. You'll be able to adjust and readjust your plan until it's just right.

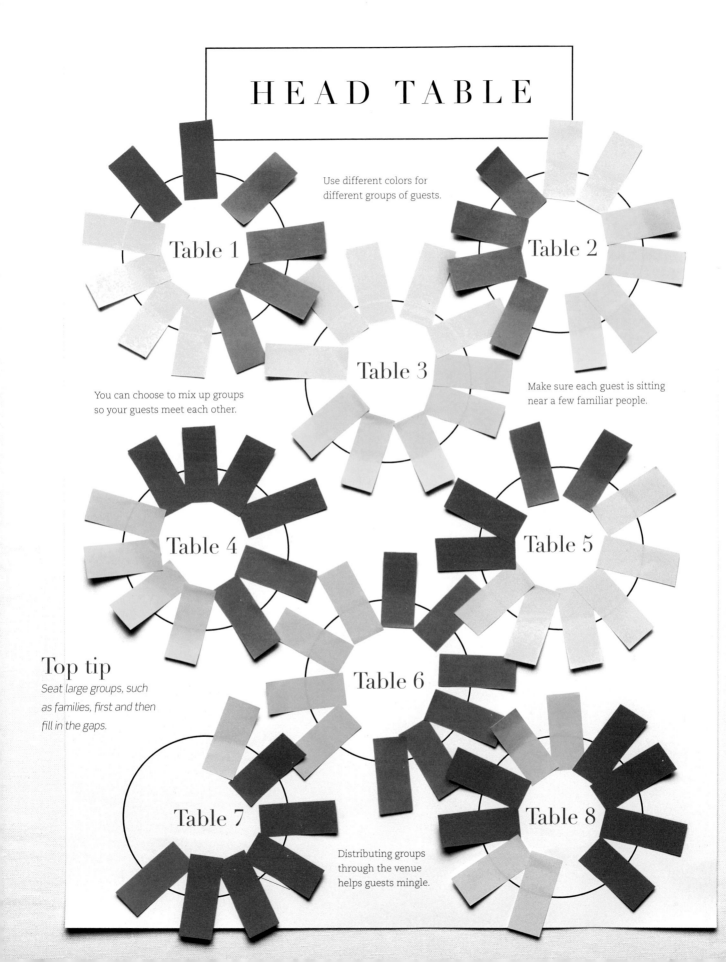

HEAD TABLE

Use different colors for different groups of guests.

Table 1

Table 2

Table 3

You can choose to mix up groups so your guests meet each other.

Make sure each guest is sitting near a few familiar people.

Table 4

Table 5

Table 6

Top tip
Seat large groups, such as families, first and then fill in the gaps.

Table 7

Table 8

Distributing groups through the venue helps guests mingle.

TABLE SETTING

PLACE THE UTENSILS in order of use, from the outside in. Forks go to the left and knives and spoons go to the right. At a formal setting, the dessert spoon and fork go at the top.

Informal

Formal

NAPKIN FOLDING

BEAUTIFULLY FOLDED NAPKINS are the perfect finishing touch for place settings. Follow these classic styles. Be sure to iron the napkins before and after folding.

ENVELOPE

1. Place the napkin on your work surface like a diamond.

2. Fold in the right-hand side to the center of the napkin.

3. Fold in the left-hand side to the center, slightly covering the tip of the triangle.

4. Fold up the bottom into the center, partially over so it is overlapping the triangle underneath.

5. Fold down the top of the napkin to make it look like an envelope.

POCKET

1. Place the napkin as a square. Fold down the top to the center.

2. Fold the bottom up to the center, slightly overlapping the fold below.

3. Flip the napkin over.

4. Fold the left edge inward, followed by the right edge to meet in the middle.

5. Fold in half to create the pocket.

LOVER'S KNOT

1. Place the napkin as a square. Fold it in half.

2. Fold it in half and then again in half, to form a long strip.

3. Fold the right-hand end down.

4. Flip the napkin over. Fold the right-hand end down to create two legs.

5. & 6. Fold leg a over to the left. Lift leg b up and over, so that it sits on top of leg a.

TRIANGLE

1. Place the napkin like a diamond. Fold it in half.

2. Fold in the top right and top left corners to form a diamond shape.

3. From the center, fold the right side and the left side out partway.

4. Flip the napkin over.

5. & 6. Fold the right-hand and left-hand flaps into the center to form a diamond shape. Fold the top point down and flip the napkin over.

REHEARSAL DINNER

THE PERFECT OPPORTUNITY to thank the wedding party and to spend time with your friends and family, the rehearsal dinner is now an established tradition.

Your wedding day is fast approaching, and the excitement and anticipation is gaining pace. Many couples choose to hold a rehearsal of the ceremony the day before their big day. A rehearsal dinner follows—it is the perfect opportunity to spend time with your guests in a relaxed setting.

WHO SHOULD HOST?

Tradition dictates that the groom's parents host the rehearsal dinner, seeing as how the bride's parents traditionally foot the bill for the wedding. But with many couples paying for their own weddings, the couple themselves, or other family members and close friends may host the dinner instead.

WHO SHOULD BE INVITED?

In addition to everyone in the wedding party who attended the ceremony rehearsal, many couples invite other family members, such as siblings and grandparents, close friends, and those who have traveled to attend the wedding. Formal invitations aren't necessary, but advance notice should be given to all who are invited.

WHEN SHOULD IT BE HELD?

The rehearsal dinner is traditionally held the evening before the wedding day, but it can be a brunch or lunch, too. If you opt for dinner in the evening, make sure you set an end time to the night to ensure that everyone gets a good night's sleep.

WHAT TYPE OF DINNER?

The dinner is an opportunity for you to mingle with your guests. It should therefore be a relaxed and intimate affair, where people can walk around and chat freely. Be it a six-course banquet or a local restaurant serving local fare, a pig roast or barbecue or picnic, it should have a different feel and ambience from the wedding.

THEMES AND SEATING PLANS

Some couples like to have a theme for their rehearsal dinner, but it should by no means steal the spotlight from the main event. Depending on the number of people you plan to invite, you might want a seating plan—a useful way to help guests meet others and encourage them to talk before the wedding.

SPEECHES AND TOASTS

Some couples and their families like to make speeches at the rehearsal dinner, while others prefer to save them for the wedding reception. The hosts often give a speech to welcome the guests, and there will generally be someone who raises their glass to toast the happy couple at least once during the evening. The bride and groom often take this opportunity to make a speech together to thank their family and friends for their help and support. It is at the rehearsal dinner that, traditionally, gifts are presented to the bridesmaids, groomsmen, and parents.

PERSONAL TOUCHES

The rehearsal dinner is an intimate event, and some couples choose to share images and videos of special moments from their life together. It's the perfect opportunity for the bride and groom to take stock of everything that's gone before, before they part ways to meet the next day at the ceremony and embark on their married life together, making many more memories.

Enjoy a relaxed meal with friends and family before the big day.

WEDDING DAY TIME LINE

YOUR BIG DAY has finally arrived. To help the day run smoothly write a clear time line for the whole day. Make sure you have a few copies printed out and a list of contact numbers for the key members of the bridal party, the makeup artist, the hair stylist, the venue, the caterer, the photographer, and the florist. With the maid of honor and the best man keeping everyone on track, you can sit back, relax, and enjoy the most wonderful day of your life!

Getting ready

Breakfast It's important you start the day off with a decent breakfast. Avoid any foods that might make you bloated or uncomfortable in your dress. The groom should also make sure he and his groomsmen eat well too. **Hair and makeup** Whether you're headed to the salon or getting your hair and makeup done at home, now is the time to get it taken care of. Make sure enough time has been factored into this part of your day. **Get dressed** It's time for the bridesmaids to get their dresses on and for you to get into your wedding dress. The groom and groomsmen should already be dressed in their tuxes or suits and headed to the ceremony venue. **Ready to roll** Your bridal car or other form of transportation should have arrived. Get your shoes on and don't forget your bouquet!

Your special day

Your ceremony Now's the time to say "I do." **Say "cheese"** The official photos usually follow right after the ceremony. **Champagne and appetizers** While the bride and groom are whisked off by the photographer for the portrait shots, the guests are served drinks and light snacks. **Wedding reception** This is usually a sit-down meal that takes a few hours from start to finish. **Speeches and toasts** are either done before or after the meal, depending on when you schedule them. **Cutting the cake** The tradition is for the couple to cut their cake and eat a slice each. **First dance** Kick-start the evening with your first dance as a married couple. Dance the night away before you head off on your honeymoon.

Wedding favors

WEDDING FAVORS are commonly given to every guest at a wedding. They are a token gesture to say thank you to your guests for making the effort to attend.

Often the favors are put on each place setting. They can be as inexpensive or as extravagant as your budget allows. If you don't have the budget or don't feel it's necessary, then you don't have to have favors. Don't feel that you have to give too much. It's not worth blowing your budget. You can often get discounts if you order items in bulk, such as chocolates, and then portion them out into nice presentation boxes.

HELP IS AT HAND

Brides can ask their bridesmaids to get together before the big day to assemble the favors. It can be an incredibly daunting and time-consuming task to do on your own.

WELCOME BAGS

If you have guests coming to your wedding from far away then welcome bags can be placed in their hotel rooms as a way to say hello and show your appreciation.

GIFTS FOR THE BRIDAL PARTY

It's essential to say thank you to your bridal party, parents, and anyone else who has played an important role in helping you plan your big day. The groom will traditionally say thank yous in his speech and this can be the ideal moment to give the gifts to the individuals. Another popular time is at the rehearsal dinner the night before the wedding. Here are some ideas for what you can give:

• Flowers
• Necklace or bracelet. If you'd like the bridesmaids to wear them at the wedding then give them the night before.
• Engraved gift
• Locket or brooch
• Wine
• Handbag
• Stuffed animal for a flower girl or ring bearer
• Luxury chocolates

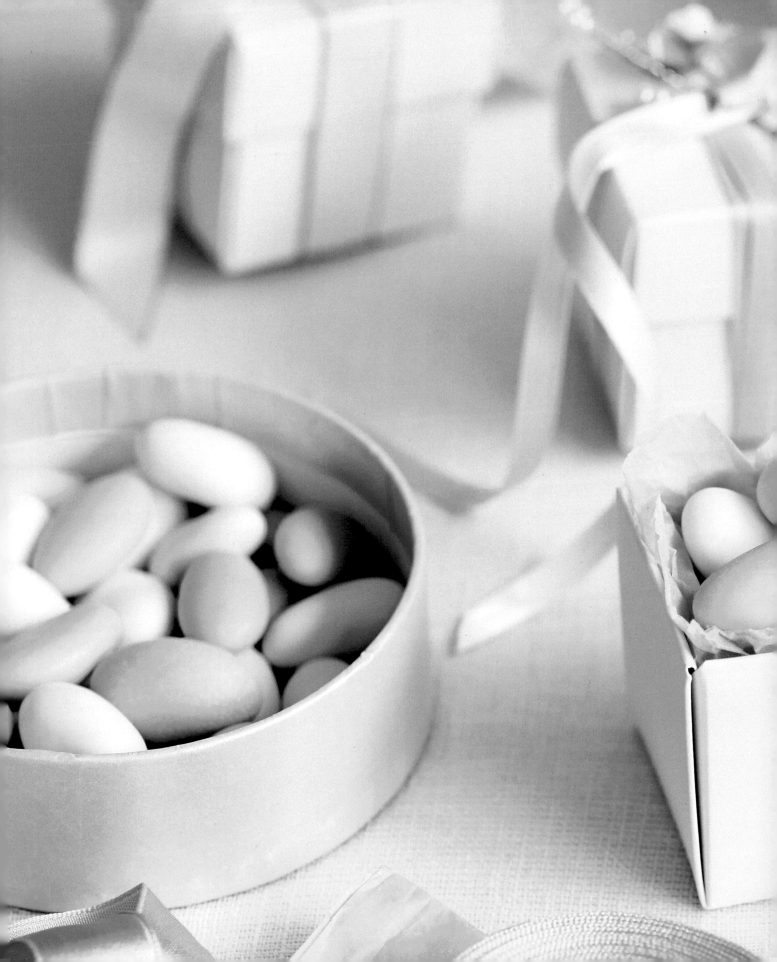

THANK-YOU CARDS

EARLY WEDDING GIFTS should be acknowledged before the big day. Thank-you cards should be mailed out two to three weeks after the bridal shower and up to 12 weeks after the wedding, although this can be later if you're on a particularly long honeymoon.

Thank you for coming to our wedding.

• Don't forget to thank people for the role they performed on the day.

• If a person has attended more than one event then you need to give them separate thank-you notes for each event.

• Remember to use your maiden name on any cards that are sent out before the wedding.

• The bride traditionally writes the thank-you notes, but practically it helps if the groom does his fair share.

• When thanking a guest for a monetary gift do not state the amount, but do mention how you intend to use the money—for help toward the honeymoon or wedding itself.

• Choose stationary that fits the theme of your wedding.

• Traditional etiquette denotes that you mention the actual gift in your thank-you card or note.

• Make your thank-you notes warm and personal.

• Write a list as you go along, either in a notebook or on your computer. Cards and tags can easily get mislaid. Make a note of the giver, the gift, the registry where it was bought, and the date when you mailed out your thank-you card.

Congratulations!

YOU DID IT! You finally tied the knot. Congratulations on all your planning and hard work to create such a spectacular and memorable day. Here's to your life as a married couple!

Just married

INDEX

*"For **true** love is inexhaustible; the more you give, the more you have."*

- Charles-Augustin Sainte-Beuve

With thanks

The publisher would like to thank: Photographers Andy Crawford and Dave King, proofreaders Jennifer Lane and Lee Wilson, production editor Rebecca Fallowfield, indexer Marie Lorimer, design assistant Stefan Georgiou, freelance editor Niki Foreman, Pip Jenkins for the use of her garden, and Heather Sandlin for writing sales material and assisting at photo shoots.

Additionally, we'd like to thank the Abigail Bloom Cake Company for lending us their beautiful wedding cakes.

www.theabigailbloomcakecompany.com

We'd also like to thank photographer Ruth Jenkinson for the use of her photograph on pages 192–193 and wedding photographer Martins Kikulis for the use of his photographs on page 197.

www.martinskikulis.com

Finally, thank you to Mark and Laura Cullen and Thomas and Kathryn Mann for allowing us to include photographs from their weddings.

About the florists

DK would like to thank the fabulous Mark Welford and Stephen Wicks for all the beautiful flowers they supplied for this book. They opened their flower shop, Bloomsbury Flowers, in London in 1994. Their mission was to make the arrangements as theatrical as possible, but also to keep them simple and classic. You can find out more about their gorgeous creations at: www.bloomsburyflowers.co.uk